GAME

Edible

Series Editor: Andrew F. Smith

EDIBLE is a revolutionary new series of books dedicated to food and drink that explores the rich history of cuisine. Each book reveals the global history and culture of one type of food or beverage.

Already published

Apple Erika Janik *Beef* Lorna Piatti-Farnell *Bread* William Rubel *Cake* Nicola Humble *Caviar* Nichola Fletcher *Champagne* Becky Sue Epstein *Cheese* Andrew Dalby *Chocolate* Sarah Moss and Alexander Badenoch *Cocktails* Joseph M. Carlin *Curry* Colleen Taylor Sen *Dates* Nawal Nasrallah *Game* Paula Young Lee *Gin* Lesley Jacobs Solmonson *Hamburger* Andrew F. Smith *Herbs* Gary Allen *Hot Dog* Bruce Kraig *Ice Cream* Laura B. Weiss *Lemon* Toby Sonneman *Lobster* Elisabeth Townsend *Milk* Hannah Velten *Mushroom* Cynthia D. Bertelsen *Offal* Nina Edwards *Olive* Fabrizia Lanza *Oranges* Clarissa Hyman *Pancake* Ken Albala *Pie* Janet Clarkson *Pineapple* Kaori O'Connor *Pizza* Carol Helstosky *Pork* Katharine M. Rogers *Potato* Andrew F. Smith *Rum* Richard Foss *Salmon* Nicolaas Mink *Sandwich* Bee Wilson *Soup* Janet Clarkson *Spices* Fred Czarra *Tea* Helen Saberi *Whiskey* Kevin R. Kosar *Wine* Marc Millon

Game

A Global History

Paula Young Lee

REAKTION BOOKS

This book is dedicated to the animals that feed us

Published by Reaktion Books Ltd
33 Great Sutton Street
London EC1V 0DX, UK
www.reaktionbooks.co.uk

First published 2013

Printed and bound in China
by Toppan Printing Co. Ltd.

A catalogue record for this book is available from the British Library

ISBN 978 1 78023 170 9

Contents

Introduction

In his *Grand dictionnaire de cuisine* (1873), the French novelist Alexandre Dumas *père* observed that the Chinese and wealthy Germans were very fond of eating the front paws of bears. This dish was also a culinary delicacy in Moscow, where Dumas had travelled as part of a gastronomic tour of Russia. There he met the French chef Urbain Dubois, who had mastered its preparation during his service at the court of Prince Alexei Fedorovich Orloff. According to Dumas, this was Dubois' recipe:

> Begin with the paws, which are sold pre-skinned, then wash them, salt them, and place them in a casserole and cover with a vinegar marinade. Leave them there for two or three days. Put bacon and ham slices as well as a bed of vegetables in a pan, put the paws on this bed, and cover them with broth. Cook it for seven or eight hours on very low heat, adding broth as it is reduced.

As soon as they were cooked, the paws were cooled, cut in four pieces, seasoned with cayenne pepper and coated with melted butter, then returned to the oven for a half hour. They were served with spicy sauce and currant jelly.

Bear steaks were still common in nineteenth-century Russia, but they were fast becoming rarities in the food shops of Paris. The prized meat could still be obtained in the capital city, Dumas sighed, but you had to know which purveyors carried it. Much like cocaine and absinthe, this disreputable substance wasn't illegal during Dumas' lifetime, but its consumption was a sign of bohemianism, a mode of living that defied bourgeois conventions. A taste for the outré was a symptom of the true artistic temperament, for an aesthetic sensibility was required to appreciate strong flavours that would otherwise offend the senses.

Bear meat is no longer commercially available in France, where the once-plentiful brown bear has disappeared. Its sale is illegal in many countries, including the United States, but it can be shared. As a child growing up in Maine, I ate bear paw dropped round by neighbours. The biggest impression it made on me was that it wasn't squishy like Spam. It also didn't come in a pretty tin, and it couldn't be purchased at the A&P supermarket. Like pie, peas and bread, it was homemade. In my six-year-old brain, this was make-it-yourself meat.

Prior to the Industrial Age, traditional game animals were chiefly members of the deer family (including elk, moose and reindeer), rabbits and hares, and birds such as duck and partridge. Game meat resulted when these animals were taken by hunting. Today, however, these same animals are routinely farmed: they neither live in the wild, nor is their meat the product of the hunt. The definition of game has both expanded and contracted, so that all wild animals are subject to regulation as potential game, but few animals qualify as such. The u.s. legal definition applies: 'The only manner in which a private individual can acquire ownership in game is by possessing it lawfully such as by hunting and killing it under a license.' It is the law, and not the character of the animal, that places it

Half-human monsters, from Konrad von Megenberg, *Buch der natur* (1481), first written *c.* 1349.

under the rubric of 'game'. Thus, for example, in the state of Texas it is legal to hunt Bigfoot, also known as Sasquatch. It is illegal in California, as Bigfoot has not been defined by the state's Fish and Game Code as a non-game mammal, and its (unconfirmed, hypothetical) populations are, according to the California Department of Fish and Game, too small for a hunting season on them to be considered.

In the modern era, game is legally defined. Today in Europe and North America, as well as in extremely limited parts of South America and North Africa, familiar game animals include boar and deer, as well as small game such as hare, duck and goose. A mere century ago, however, hunters in these same regions pursued non-traditional game birds such as pelicans, cormorants and bitterns. Imperial Romans feasted on flamingos and parrots. Ancient Egyptians enjoyed striped hyena. In short, until the rise of the slaughterhouse made beef, pork and chicken cheap and widely available, humans ate nearly every bird and animal they could scavenge or catch, even the ones that didn't taste very good.

In agricultural economies where hunters kill to eat, game meat is frequently attached to generational poverty. In industrialized nations, the practice of hunting is cast as an anachronistic exercise in cruelty. Though game meat can be delicious, it's unpredictable. It tastes of wildness. Irregular in texture and taste, game meat is the flesh of a unique yet nameless creature. It confesses its life directly to the tongue, for the animal's age, sex, temperament and stress levels directly affect its flavour. Thus the Victorian-era doyenne of household management, Mrs Isabella Beeton, recommended choosing a British buck taken between 'June and Michaelmas', and a doe between November and January, for this is when their

Currier & Ives, *American Dead Game* print, 1866.

Udo Keppler, *Dives and Lazarus: Fed with the Crumbs Which Fell from the Rich Man's Table*, 1910, satirical print.

respective flesh reaches its 'ideal perfection'. In order to prepare the meat, the chef needs to know these details, including the most uncomfortable fact of all: whether the animal died well.

It is a mark of civilized people that they prefer not to think about such things, and Mrs Beeton was no exception. She deemed hunters 'rude' specimens of 'manliness', whose devotion to the chase was quite possibly proof that they were suffering from 'madness'. Her husband, a London publisher of women's magazines, did not hunt. Mrs Beeton ran a household with servants, and died at the age of 28. In her girlish imagination, the ideal world of the future would be domesticated, and hunting would be 'the amusement of the opulent'. Implicitly this would occur because agricultural production would fill all bellies, magically bearing no relationship to unpalatable realities such as exploitative farm labour, the systemic sacrifice of wildlife habitat to create arable fields, the extermination of cute pests such as sparrows and bunnies or the nastier sides of British imperialism.

A century and a half later, she is close to getting her wish. True game meats have become gastronomic rarities chiefly available to indigenous peoples such as the Inuit, the rural poor and the economic elite. It has become the ultimate food of social extremes. Predictably game meat has also become a sign of morality, invested with religious symbolism even as it is condemned as a sign of decadence. 'For years, as a child', writes Sy Montgomery in *Birdology* (2010), 'I had believed that venery was one of the seven deadly sins, like envy, greed, and sloth.' But 'venery' has two meanings, only one of which referred to the 'pleasures of the bed'. In 1813, this was *Webster's Dictionary*'s way of referring to sexual intercourse, reflecting the etymological derivation of the word, 'venery', from the Latin *veneria*, the root of which is *venus* (love). The other meaning of venery refers to 'the practice or sport of hunting and the chase'. It comes from the Latin *vēnārī*, to hunt, which yielded the French word *vénerie*, and from there, *venison*.

Unfortunately, 'venery' is spelled the same in English whether its etymological roots are lodged in *venus* (love) or *vēnārī* (to hunt). And thus begins the confusion that still haunts the term today, mingling venality with venison inside horrified brains. Though it's impossible to tell from the title, Joseph Howe's *Excessive Venery, Masturbation, and Continence* (1883), doesn't wail about too much hunting but about too much sex. The shelves of public libraries are still crammed with quaint books warning of the 'dangerous effects of secret and excessive venery', such as Samuel Tissot's *Onanism* (1766). This backdrop of moral condemnation gives Mrs Beeton's Victorian distaste for the hunt a whole new cast. As Giovanni Boccaccio had noted in his *Decameron* (*c*. 1349–53), men suffering from lovesickness 'have many ways of relief': they can go hunting, hawking or fishing. Today, when men who hunt become men who *love* hunting, they're cast as perverts dedicated to yet another nasty activity conducted, suspiciously, in solitude.

Over three centuries, the bear paw has gone from being a prized delicacy worthy of emperors, to taboo fodder that makes sensitive souls shudder. The change in gastronomic status has nothing to do with its palatability, and everything to do with dwindling natural resources and the disappearing wilderness. The loss of wildlife habitat means that game meat is increasingly becoming a luxury available only to those who can afford to purchase it. On a certain level, this has always been the case. The daily fare served at the palace of King Solomon consisted of 'ten head of stall-fed cattle, twenty of pasture-fed cattle and a hundred sheep and goats, as well as deer, gazelles, roebucks and choice fowl' (1 Kings 4:23). The fabled banquets of royalty ranging from the sixteenth-century roasts of Henry VIII to the Manchu Han banquet held for the Kangxi Emperor of the Qing dynasty featured menus that cannot replicated today, because many of the wild animals that were served are now endangered or extinct. The Manchu Han menu reportedly included leopard foetuses, rhinoceros tails, deer tendons and the front paws of bears taken in autumn, because it is then that the paws are most fat and tasty.

These delicacies illuminate the culinary expression of political power expressed through extraordinary waste. The *Uniwersalna książka kucharska*, often called the 'bible of Polish cooking', notes that 'at royal banquets, a favourite dish was a pâté made of peacocks' brains, and two to three thousand had to be slaughtered at one time.' But it is both the nature of the parts being consumed as well as the quantities that makes one cringe, much like the 1.25 billion chicken wings served up in 2012 for the playoffs of the American football champ - ionship game called, fittingly, the Super Bowl. That, too, is extraordinary power, and extraordinary waste. It is partly in reaction to fast-food popularity that game meat is now re-entering the world of gastronomy, a domain defined by and still dominated by the French. One word sums it up: ortolan.

Ortolan (*Emberiza hortulana*) is a tiny songbird in the bunting family. Physically it resembles a small sparrow. A coveted delicacy, it commands exorbitant prices. It's also illegal to hunt in France. Globally the ortolan is neither endangered nor threatened. It's just so delicious that French officials feared it would go the way of the Burgundy snail (*Helix pomatia*), so avidly hunted for the dish escargot that it virtually disappeared. (Though not typically thought of as game animals, snails are subject to hunting regulations in various countries. In England, for example, *H. pomatia* is protected and thus illegal to hunt.) According to Dumas, the people of Toulouse liked to fatten their ortolans before killing them by plunging their heads in 'very strong vinegar'. They were then plucked but not gutted or boned, and lightly flambéed, rubbed with a cut lemon, threaded on a skewer, covered in butter, rolled in fine

Friedrich Graetz, *A Family Party: The 200th Birthday of the Healthiest of Uncle Sam's Adopted Children*, 1883, satirical print.

Alexander Lawson, illustration from Alexander Wilson, *Birds, Nests and Eggs* (1814).

breadcrumbs and roasted over a high flame for seven or eight minutes before being served whole with wedges of lemon and crusty croutons. But the most famous method involves a bird drowned in Armagnac brandy, and a white dinner napkin tossed over the eater's head. This is allegedly how François Mitterrand, former president of France, ate the orto-lans he'd requested for his deathbed feast. Indeed, ever since ortolans have become illegal to hunt, it seems that everybody is rushing out for a plate. Celebrity chefs boast about crunching through their tiny roasted bodies, and food bloggers succumb so often to this illicit treat that their confessions border on cliché. Ironically the bird's banned status has only intensified the gourmand's desire to experience this mythic meal before it truly becomes impossible to obtain, driving up black-market prices to anywhere from £35 in Britain to U.S.$215 per bite-size bird. The economic incentive has merely attached a price tag to poaching, which never stopped in the first place because French farmers think the ban is stupid.

Consider their contempt an act of political defiance. When the Nazis occupied France, they made it a crime for people to hunt. The hunting and trapping of small game had been a cherished right of the citizenry, afforded even to peasants during the Age of Absolutism when *la chasse*, the coursing of large game (chiefly red deer, roe deer and fallow deer), was the exclusive privilege of royalty. After the Second World War ended and the Allies freed France, my brother-in-law's French grandfather used to net tiny birds and kill them by squashing their heads with his thumb. He felt he could do this because the Nazis had sent him to the concentration camps for his role as a leader of the Resistance, and he had survived even as his friends died horribly around him. After he returned home, he lived long enough as a free man to pass on the tradition of netting birds to his grandson. A songbird's life means something terribly complex when taken by such hands, which is why gastronomes declare that the ortolan represents the soul of France.

There were practical considerations to the European tradition of eating buntings, sparrows and other birds partial to seeds. As Dumas had explained, they would otherwise proliferate into clouds as 'thick as mosquitos', and devastate the wheat and grape harvests. Dumas didn't think it reasonable to deprive Parisians of their baguettes and Beaujolais out of misguided sympathy for wildlife. The French have been netting, trapping and serving songbirds at the family table for at least 1,000 years, yet it is only in the past decade that the ortolan's numbers have meaningfully declined. To be sure, poaching is a factor, but it is not the primary agent. The European Commission, the executive body that determines whether wildlife requires protected status, states that 'agricultural changes have led up to reductions in crop diversity and increases in human disturbance during the breeding season.' The threat to the ortolan doesn't come from hunters. It comes from factory farming.

An individual creature may survive the confrontation with man, but a species rarely escapes obliteration when it gets in the way of shopping malls and swimming pools. The black bear in this photograph is a taxidermied specimen. Despite appearances, the little girl is under no threat. The animal, however, is extremely dead. For wild animals, civilization brings death by a thousand hugs and kisses. A century ago, the consequences of Mrs Beeton's views were apparent

Amy Stein, *Watering Hole*, 2005.

to her contemporary, Lewis Carroll, who mocked the genteel nihilism of the bourgeoisie in his poem of 1874 about the hunting of a mysterious creature called the Snark:

> They sought it with thimbles, they sought it with care;
> They pursued it with forks and hope;
> They threatened its life with a railway-share;
> They charmed it with smiles and soap.

The stanza may be interpreted as an indictment of the march of progress as it gobbles up the land. Thanks to the incursions of heavy industry ('railway') facilitated by politics ('smiles'), prettied up by domesticity ('thimbles') and justified in the name of hunger and hygiene ('forks' and 'soap'), the Snark has disappeared from the face of the earth. Still, the joke is on us: the disappearance of the Snark also condemned the Baker to the same fate. He was a member of the hunting party that included a Butcher and a Beaver, who become unlikely best friends, and a Banker, who goes insane.

Snarks and talking beavers aren't real. But in ancient China, relates the geographer Yi-Fu Tuan, the founder of the Qin dynasty (*c.* 221–206 BCE) created a vast hunting preserve for the 'rare beasts and birds that were tributes from the vassal states'. These creatures were said to have included such oddities as rhinoceroses from Huang Chih and unicorns from Chiu Chen. Today the 'unicorns' raised by the 'Sisters at Radiant Farms' in 'County Meath, Ireland', sustain the merry tradition of keeping cryptids in managed game parks in a state of semi-domestication. When farmed in this fashion, even animals that exist primarily in the imagination are best understood as creatures of commercial forces that insist on a steady supply of uniform products destined for the marketplace. These forces submit real and invented game animals to

Eugene S. M. Haines, *The Taxidermist's After-dinner Dream: 'We Thought All Nature Subservient to Our Will'*, *c.* 1870.

the same economic, legal and regulatory constraints imposed on fully domesticated livestock such as cows and pigs. It was thus entirely predictable that, in 2010, the American law firm Faegre & Benson, acting on behalf of the National Pork Board (NPB), issued a cease-and-desist letter to the online purveyors of canned unicorn meat ('an excellent source of sparkles!'). Under threat of a lawsuit, the company, ThinkGeek.com, was ordered to stop calling their product 'the new white meat', because it was too easily confused with 'the other white meat', pork. The company responded to the warning by stating: 'We'd like to publicly apologize to the NPB for the confusion over unicorn and pork – and for their awkward extended pause on the phone after we had explained our unicorn meat doesn't actually exist.' The 'unicorn meat' supplied by Ireland's 'Radiant Farms' was a stuffed toy.

As the palate constricts, so does the imagination. Today there is only the wild animal on one side, whose status as game is legally and historically defined. On the other side there are the pathways by which it meets man; either both escape the encounter, or one dies.

I

The Hunting of the Snark: A Brief Overview of Game

In 1951 the annual Explorers Club Dinner in New York City included an appetizer made of a 'mysterious meat', labelled 'mammoth' by the newspapers. It's unclear what the meat actually was. According to Dorthea Sartain, the Explorers Club's curator of archives, the head of the dinner committee believed the meat was actually prehistoric sloth (*Megatherium*), an extinct creature the size of a modern elephant. Others disagreed, suggesting instead that the mammoth was actually a mastodon. Either way, the dish was nasty. 'I heard it was like putting a handful of mud in your mouth', club member Alfred McLaren confided to a reporter at the 2008 dinner. I have been unable to confirm a scientific find of frozen mastodon, mammoth or giant sloth in 1951, but 50 years earlier the palaeontologist Eugene Pfizenmayer had excavated the frozen remains of a mammoth (*Mammuthus primigenius*) in northeastern Siberia. Preserved muscle tissue taken from the left hind leg of the mammoth is now in the collection of the National Museum of Natural History of the Smithsonian Institution in Washington, DC, where it floats in a large glass apothecary jar filled with eau de vie. It looks like a chunk of red meat that's been sitting in the freezer for too long.

Prior to the nineteenth century, naturalists routinely tasted their finds. According to Pliny, for example, the 'goodnesse and sweetnesse' of the cuckoo could not be surpassed. Aristotle, by contrast, preferred the 'fat and palatable' flesh of hawks. In 1801 the palaeontologist Georges Cuvier remarked that every wild animal found in the Ménagerie du Jardin des Plantes in Paris, including lions, tigers and polar bears, was perfectly edible, as reported in the findings of a 'very bizarre man' who had eaten one of each. One of the few confirmed culinary experiments with an extinct game animal involved the discovery in 1979 of a mummified 36,000-year-old bison dubbed 'Blue Babe'. Palaeontologist Dale Guthrie cooked his frozen find in a stewpot with stock and vegetables. 'The meat was well aged but still a little tough', he reported, 'and it gave the stew a strong Pleistocene aroma, but nobody there would have dared miss it.' The conclusion was that the extinct bison stew was 'agreeable'.

Humans have been feasting on wild beasts long before the invention of picky eating. Before the advent of agriculture and animal husbandry, humans relied on wild meat to survive. That early humans practised hunting seems to be confirmed by the Palaeolithic cave paintings of Lascaux, France, which depict humans with simple weapons alongside modern and extinct animals such as the aurochs (an extinct bull) and the megaloceros (an extinct giant stag). Even so, the premise that Stone Age humans actively hunted large and dangerous game in 14,500 BCE is questionable, and anthropologists suggest that they scavenged the meat instead. The matter will not be resolved any time soon, but it is telling that the surviving bones in the caves of Lascaux didn't belong to giant stags but to manageably sized reindeer.

It seems that for as long as humans have been human, hunters have been making up fish stories about the size of the one that got away: there's a significant mismatch between the mythical representation of mighty cavemen bringing down woolly mammoths with spears, and the reality of the meat that got dragged back to the cave. The point is worth nuancing because it helps demonstrate the fact that meat is always charged with cultural meaning, even when it was clobbered during the Stone Age. Take, for example, the Palaeolithic cave habitation known as La Cotte de Saint Brélade in Jersey, one of the Channel Islands, a British dependency off the rocky coast of Normandy that was formerly contiguous with France. La Cotte de Saint Brélade was found to hold bones of woolly mammoth and woolly rhinoceros, confirming that they were eaten by Neanderthals (*Homo neanderthalensis*). Inconveniently, both these prehistoric cavemen and the guests at the Explorers Club Dinner in 1951 had obtained their meat in more or less the same way: by stumbling on to it.

As argued by Katharine Scott, now a Fellow at St Cross College, University of Oxford, the Neanderthal method consisted of driving the mammoths off cliffs, watching them smash on the rocks below, and then running down and carving up the carcasses. This supremely practical technique is a prehistoric version of staging a roadkill. It works very well, but it's not heroic in the least. The popular imagination prefers to cast the caveman as a brave warrior with spears, because this corresponds to a particular concept of hunting for food. Running over animals does not count, and neither does dropping them off cliffs. Both of these methods are unsporting.

Depending on the laws in your part of the world, smashed meat can be salvaged, and it will be tasty if you know how to cook it. Indeed, some interpretations of the Buddha's teachings affirm that roadkill is a 'pure' food because the animal died by accident. As such it is a spiritually healthy addition to the diet. By contrast, Buddhist monks are forbidden to eat animals expressly slaughtered for human consumption, such as beef cattle or broiler chickens. They are also discouraged from eating certain animals irrespective of how they lost their lives – elephants, horses, dogs and wild predators such as snakes, lions, tigers, panthers, bears and hyenas – because eating them invites their relatives to have the favour returned, and they will come to dinner expecting you to feed them.

For completely different reasons, the Judaeo-Christian tradition prohibits eating many of the same creatures, plus camels, hares and hyraxes, to name a few. According to the Torah, it is permissible to consume certain animals, and the relevant biblical passages have been interpreted to include both *b'hayma* (domesticated) and *chaya* (wild) relatives within the same species. 'These are the beasts which ye shall eat', states Deuteronomy 14:5: 'the ox, the sheep, and the goat, the hart, and the roebuck, and the fallow deer, and the wild goat, and the pygarg, and the wild ox, and the chamois'. The first three animals are straightforward, because oxen, sheep and goats have been fully domesticated for centuries, and their meat becomes beef, mutton and chevon respectively. The other seven present classificatory muddles that have vexed generations of Bible scholars. These seven are both kosher and game.

'To ascertain the natural history of the Bible is a hopeless case', commented British theologian Adam Clarke in his *Commentary on the Bible* (1831). 'Of a few of its animals and vegetables we are comparatively certain, but of the great majority we know almost nothing.' The biblical roebuck (in Hebrew, יבצ, *tsebi*), he explains, is not a roe deer but is 'generally supposed to be the antelope'. Its flesh is 'good and well flavoured'. The 'fallow deer' (רומחי, *yachmur*) is not the fallow deer, but the bubalus, or buffalo. It is 'not considered very delicious, yet in the countries where it abounds it is eaten as frequently by all classes of persons as the ox is in England'. The wild ox (ואת, *teo*), Clarke continues, is not an ox but an oryx.

Sidney Hall, 'Camelopardalis, Tarandus and Custos Messium', in
Jehoshaphat Aspin, *A Familiar Treatise on Astronomy* (1825). Astronomical
chart showing a giraffe (Camelopardalis), shepherd and reindeer forming
the constellations.

The pygarg (דישן, *dishon*) is a mystery because the word pygarg
(in Greek, πυγαργος) means 'white buttocks'. But nearly everyone who has tackled the question, Clarke included, agrees
that the biblical pygarg is not the 'pygarg, or white tail'd
Eagle' identified by seventeenth-century ornithologist Francis
Willughby, but probably refers to some kind of quadruped.
The African addax seems a likely candidate, as this screwhorn
antelope has white hindquarters in the winter.

Further complicating matters, Clarke was using the King
James translation of the Bible. In the Darby Bible, the pygarg
becomes a 'bishon'. In the New American Standard Bible,
the pygarg is an 'ibex'. And in the Douay Bible, the chamois
becomes a 'camelopardalus', or camel-leopard, otherwise
known as a giraffe. If the number of 'Is giraffe meat kosher?'
articles bouncing around the Web is any indication, this seems
to have become the standard translation of זמר, *zemer*. Crucially,

giraffes, ibex, addax and other game animals may be kosher in their living state and thus eligible for *shechitah* (ritual slaughter by a specially trained butcher known as a *shochet*) in observance of Jewish dietary laws. But while it is possible for a wild animal to be both game and kosher, it is virtually impossible for *meat* to be both, because it unites incompatible concepts.

In order to qualify as such, kosher meat must be produced via ritual slaughter of a kosher animal according to the Halaka, which disqualifies any animal that died by accident, from disease, in the course of the hunt or by any other means except the religiously sanctioned one. All seven of the wild animals listed in Deuteronomy have either antlers or horns, and most are imposing in size. They may not be as glamorous as carnivorous predators, but wild herbivores are very difficult to subdue manually, and this is a necessary step in order to subject them to the sacrificial knife. An oryx is a ruminant with fully split hooves, and thus a kosher beast. Yet it will never pass through the necessary rite to become kosher meat, because the scimitar-horned oryx (*Oryx dammah*) is nearly extinct in the wild, and other kinds of oryx are protected by secular laws. As is the case with the giraffe, the question of whether the oryx's meat is kosher is best understood as a thought experiment.

In brief, game animals become meat the way that all animals do: by the intervention of cultural, religious and legal rules between the quarry and the plate. It's just a question of which rules get applied, because they're shifting all the time. Even something as seemingly obvious as 'meat' (the flesh of animals) versus 'fish' (the flesh of fish) represents a host of cultural decisions. An animal isn't a fish, except when it is. In 1704 Michel Sarrazin, the chief physician in 'New France' (that is, Canada), petitioned the Royal Academy of Sciences in Paris to declare that the beaver's tail was fish. This eminent scientific body responded by ruling exactly as you'd expect:

yes, the beaver's tail is fish. The Faculty of Divinity at the University of Paris approved the ruling. In this peculiar matter science and religion were in complete agreement.

For all its apparent absurdities, the decision made practical sense. As noted by historian Peter C. Newman, eighteenth-century European fur traders would take beaver pelts for profit, after which they pounded the meat with 'wild fruit, then dipped the mixture into tallow and packed it into hot deer bladders for a delicious repast'. Beavers were also hunted avidly by native tribes, which valued them for fur and food. A Blackfoot legend tells of an old man who was so fond of beaver meat that his son worried he would meet with misfortune, for these animals were endowed with magic powers. Both native peoples and European trappers relied on beaver meat to survive, but only Catholics were obliged to abstain from meat during the 40-day period of Lent. For this reason, the beaver wasn't the only animal that became a fish when the bellies of devout Catholics began to rumble. Faced with similar difficulties during the age of colonization, European missionaries in South America asked the Vatican to declare the capybara a fish. Resembling an enormous guinea pig, this wild 'water pig' has webbing between its toes. This feature was enough to convince the Vatican to grant a special dispensation to its South American outposts. Centuries later, the capybara is a traditional Easter treat in Venezuela, where it graces Lenten tables in the manner of a Christmas goose.

From a zoological standpoint, the capybara is not a bird, an egg, a vegetable or a fish. It's a rodent. But tradition trumps taxonomy, and every spring, South American game hunters continue to pursue wild and ranched capybaras in anticipation of the demands of Holy Week. It is also eaten year-round as jerky and in burritos. Venezuelans typically describe capybara meat as having a 'fishy' taste. The website Foodista.com says

Gustav Mützel, 'Capybara', from *Brehm's Life of Animals* (1927).

that its flavour is 'reminiscent of pork'. In an interview with the *New York Times* in 2007, capybara expert Rexford D. Lord declared that 'it's more like rabbit than chicken, though when dried with sea salt in Venezuela it acquires a fishy flavor.'

'We'll say it's rabbit', a prisoner suggests in James Clavell's *King Rat* (1962), a best-selling novel based on Clavell's own experiences as a prisoner of war in a Japanese camp during the Second World War. A group of American and British POWs plan to sell rat meat as rabbit on the black market to help finance an escape. The first prisoner thinks himself very clever until his friend points out that there are no rabbits in Malaya. They end up calling the rat a 'mouse deer'. A local delicacy, the mouse deer is the world's smallest extant deer species, so small that they're similar in size to adult rats. 'Hell, it's just like chickens', the prisoners exclaim cynically. So the rat becomes a deer that tastes like a bird.

Game meat does not come with labels, a fact that has routinely ended in comical kitchen catastrophes. On the benign end of the spectrum, careless cooks have thrown tantrums when they discover that they've got the wrong bird for dinner. 'One day the cook, named Thirsty John / Sent for the gosling, [but] took the swan', observed Jean de La Fontaine in his seventeenth-century fable 'The Swan and the Cook'. Both of these large, semi-domesticated birds were commonly consumed during this period. From the cook's perspective, however, these birds were prepared very differently, as geese are fatty and swan meat is dry.

A carving illustration from the *White House Cook Book* (1887) shows how easy it was for cooks to mix up game birds, especially if they weren't doing the plucking themselves. Which is the partridge and which the pheasant? Somewhat unhelpfully, we are told that they are both cleaned and trussed the same way, but only the partridge is divided into two equal parts, and 'the custom of cooking them with the heads on is going into disuse somewhat'. It is thus the plucked bird whose

Louis M. Glackens, '*Say, Honest, is He Really Gone?*', 1924. The wild animals, several wearing bandages, are looking at a lone footprint in the sand, wondering if big-game hunter Theodore Roosevelt has finally departed. A capybara is visible in the centre.

head has been lopped off. By contrast, the cookbook explains, pheasants are still roasted with their heads on, but when brought to table, the heads are tucked underneath with a skewer. Correspondingly, the blind pheasant's head pops up by the wing, giving the bird the air of a mutant rubber ducky.

In France, popular plays known as *vaudevilles* mocked the practice of selling fraudulent meat to customers who were easily fooled. In *Les Cuisines parisiennes* (1843) by Dupeuty and Cormon, a customer admires a cat, calling it a hare (*lièvre*), and the cat/hare switcheroo goes on from there. In eighteenth-century France, historian Rebecca Spang relates, a vendor went on trial for selling cats to restaurants and calling them hares. Indeed, the practice was so commonplace that 'in Europe even today much of the traditional roast hare is caught in the alley', commented Joseph Vehling in 1936, 'and it belongs to a feline species. "Roof hare"', he concludes crisply, quite unbothered by the deception. There's an easy fix, but it's not for the squeamish: in Missouri, where no state laws prevent trappers from selling raccoon meat, raccoons are sold with their heads and three paws removed. 'They leave the paw on to prove it's not a cat or a dog', a satisfied customer noted in the *Kansas City Star* in 2009.

Under extraordinary circumstances, however, the cat might be served up as a cat, with no attempt at subterfuge. This was the case in 1870, when the Siege of Paris left people starving, and so they ate the zoo. A restaurant menu from the 99th day of the siege offered gourmet delights such as elephant consommé and kangaroo stew, as well as haunch of wolf with roe deer sauce. Technically, however, these meats were exotic but not game, because no hunting was involved in their making. Instead the animals' managed status as zoo animals made them 'public pets', to borrow the historian Harriet Ritvo's phrase, which is why their consumption was shocking. The signal dish

'Come in, Ladies and Gentlemen', French caricature showing 'rosbif' (roast beef) being served that is actually cat, early 18th century.

on this menu of zoological cuisine was 'cat flanked by rats' (*le chat flanqué de rats*), because it openly challenged taboos that exempted pets from being food. It was not a euphemism for *langue de chat* (literally 'cat's tongue'), a buttery biscuit beloved by schoolchildren, but a frank admission of wartime culinary pragmatism. Unapologetically, the 'cat' was cat, and the other meat was rat.

In this topsy-turvy environment, some French chefs sneakily served 'elephant' that was actually horsemeat, but cooks on tight budgets typically valued creativity over cheating. The written record is full of recipes that promote clever meat deceptions, such as mock turtle soup, made out of boiled calf's head, or *mouton à la chasseur* (hunter's mutton), which is mutton prepared to taste like venison. The *Ménagier de Paris* (1393) even provides instructions for how 'to Counterfeit Bear Venison from a Piece of Beef':

> Take flank, and let it be chopped in large chunks as for loin stew, then parboil, lard and roast: and then boil a boar's tail, and let your meat boil a little, and throw sauce and all in a dish.

The amiable patterns of deception found in medieval and early modern recipe books typically confirm the meat of large game as the higher-status food, with cheaper, domesticated meats such as beef and mutton being substituted for the more elusive 'venison' of bear and deer. (A leg of mutton boiled and served 'like venison', notes Hannah Glasse in *The Art of Cookery Made Plain and Easy* of 1747, is a 'genteel dish for a first course'.) By the late Industrial Age, however, this pattern of valuation had changed, with game meat becoming increasingly steeped in sad narratives of deprivation. Between 1856 and 1859, British geographer and explorer Sir Richard Francis Burton travelled from Zanzibar to Lake Tanganyika and back, and wrote *The Lake Regions of Central Africa: A Picture of Exploration*. Burton had this to say about people's love of meat in Eastern Africa:

> The crave for meat is satisfied by eating almost every description of living thing, clean or unclean; as a rule,

Fried meat of African animals. Left to right: venison sausage, kudu, ostrich, springbok, crocodile. Restaurant Mama Africa, Capetown, 2012.

however, the East African prefers beef, which strangers find flatulent and heating. Like most people, they reject game when they can command the flesh of tame beasts.

As with any blanket cultural generalization, the passage should be taken with a grain of salt. The assessment chiefly confirms that Burton viewed livestock beef as a status symbol among East Africans, and found himself superior for being able to afford it. Burton also notes that 'the cheapest and vilest meat is mutton', and the 'favourite' game meat is zebra: 'it is smoked or jerked, despite which it retains a most savoury flavour'. Fine restaurants in Africa still offer zebra meat, and it is affirmed to be exceptionally good. Today's recipes suggest substituting beef when zebra is not available.

The oldest surviving European cookbook, *De opsoniis et condimentis sive arte coquinaria, Libri decem* (Ten books of soups and sauces), compiled around the end of the fourth century CE or at the beginning of the fifth, likewise tossed together the meat of wild and domesticated animals with no sense of transgression. Written around the first century, supposedly by a certain Apicius, this cookbook grouped the meat of domestic livestock and game animals together under the heading 'quadrupeds', an eclectic group that included wild boar, pig, wild sheep, kid goats, gazelles and dormice. The free interplay between wild and domesticated meats persisted up to the beginnings of the slaughterhouse as a municipal mechanism for making meat. According to the eighteenth-century *Encyclopédie* of Denis Diderot and Jean le Rond d'Alembert, 'white meat' (*viande blanche*) referred to veal and chicken; 'dark meat' included hare, venison and boar; 'small meat' came from snared animals; and 'big meat' was beef. There wasn't a word for game meat. It just wasn't 'meat meat' (*viande viande*), which was the flesh of domesticated animals raised specifically for human consumption, such as certain cows and sheep.

It can be argued that 'meat meat' was fairly low in the food hierarchy prior to the Industrial Age. 'Apicius, the most gluttonous gorger of all spendthrifts, established the view that the flamingo's tongue has a specially fine flavour', Pliny observed in his *Natural History*. The *Historia Augusta* (Augustan History) relates that the tyrant Elagabalus, who become emperor aged fourteen and was assassinated at seventeen,

> frequently ate camels-heels and also cockscombs taken from the living birds, and the tongues of peacocks and nightingales . . . He served to the palace-attendants, moreover, huge platters heaped up with the viscera of mullets, and flamingo-brains, partridge-eggs, thrush-brains, and the heads of parrots, pheasants and peacocks.

A fascinating compilation of real and fake emperors, *Historia Augusta* mixes together facts and fiction in the manner of a supermarket tabloid. Composed sometime before 425 CE, and of disputed authorship, it remains an unreliable source for biographical information, but serves as an excellent reference regarding the cultural role of food as a measure of imperial decadence. At one memorable feast, Elagabalus served wild sows' udders and rice mixed with real pearls, but one of the most infamous banquets was hosted by Lucius Verus, who served a variety of meats to his guests and then gave them the 'live animals either tame or wild, winged or quadruped, of whatever kind were the meats that were served'.

Centuries later, the high culinary status assigned to cox-combs and tongues can be understood via the example of a sumptuous meal described by René Auguste Constantin de Renneville, a French Protestant in a Catholic country during the seventeenth-century reign of Louis XIV. To escape religious persecution, he decamped to the Netherlands. When he returned to France, he ended up imprisoned in the Bastille, which held political prisoners as well as struggling writers suspected of being spies. Because they weren't common criminals, the Bastille's prisoners could pay to improve the quality of their food. Memorably, Renneville once enjoyed a seven-course meal served by the turnkey, who also played the roles of waiter and sommelier. This meal included a pea soup garnished with lettuce, a 'quarter of fowl' followed by a plate of juicy beef-steak, with plenty of gravy and a sprinkling of parsley, and on another plate, 'a quarter of forcemeat pie well stuffed with sweetbreads [pancreas and lymph nodes], cock's combs, aspara-gus, mushrooms, and truffles; and in a third a ragout of sheep's tongue, the whole excellently cooked'. As a starving writer, Renneville was even more thrilled by the fact that the Sun King paid for his expensive meal.

Forcemeat is a mixture of finely ground or pounded meats, typically pork, seafood, poultry or liver, and also game such as venison, boar or rabbit, as well an array of game birds. In medieval Poland a similar preparation was called *zrazy*, as in *Zrazy po Cyprjsku*, Hashmeat in the Cypress Style. Wrapped in grape leaves, this particular version was served at a banquet of 1364 held in Krakow to honour King Peter of Cyprus. An anglicized version of Renneville's forcemeat pie appears as 'Chicken Pie' in Hannah Glasse's *The Art of Cookery Made Plain and Easy*, which recommends a forcemeat made of two whole pounded chickens, a pound of veal, a half-pound of suet, anchovy, egg yolk and thyme. Then take

> two sweet-breads, cut them into five or six pieces, lay them all over, season them with pepper and salt, strew over them half an ounce of truffles and morels, two or three arti-choke-bottoms cut to pieces, a few cocks-combs if you have them, [and] a palate boiled tender and cut to pieces.

This version of forcemeat pie is almost certainly blander than the one Renneville enjoyed, given that *The Art of Cookery* devoted all of its third chapter ('On How Expensive a French Cook's Sauce Is') to admonishing the French for their manner of cooking. The British way is 'the best way to make pigeon pie', the author snips, because the French stuff their pigeons first with a 'very high forcemeat' and then they 'season high'. Dismissively, she concludes: 'That is according to different palates.'

Whether French, British or Polish, these expensive speci-alities mix categories of meat (*and* poultry *and* fish *and* shell - fish) together in such a way that utterly disregards the need of moral hygienists to prevent promiscuous fleshy mingling. Not only do these meat pies fail to respect the now highly patrolled boundary between domesticated and wild, but they also defy current assumptions regarding the hierarchy of the body by placing a high value on parts that today would be rejected by all but the very hungry.

'Meat is muscle!' Philip Hasheider affirms in *The Complete Book of Butchering* (2010). Just about all of the rest of the animal is offal, including the edible skin (called 'crackling' or 'scratchings' when it's pig, and 'gribenes' in the U.S. when it's goose or chicken). Forcemeat and ground beef are both the result of intense processing, but the foods occupy opposite ends of today's symbolic hierarchy. In forcemeat, the fat is prized. In ground beef, leanness is more desirable to American home cooks, even at the expense of texture and taste. Historically the highest culinary value has been assigned to the parts that provide the most calories and nutrition: the organs in general, but especially the brains, marrow, blood and fat, this last, according to Burton, being 'the essential element of good living'.

Thus in *Nile Tributaries of Abyssinia, and the Sword Hunters of the Hamran Arabs* (1867), Samuel White Baker noted that the hippopotamus is 'extremely valuable' to Arabs, because it not only yields a workable hide and 'a large quantity of excellent flesh', but 'about two hundred pounds of fat'. Baker stressed that 'every morsel of the flesh has been stored either by the natives or for our own use; and whenever we have had a good supply of antelope or giraffe meat, I have avoided firing a shot at the hippo.' But it is his lengthy and detailed description of elephant fat which underscores its value. He personally dislikes the meat, finding it 'exceedingly strong and disagreeable', but acknowledges that the Arabs have a special fondness for it, finding it 'fat and juicy'. Both he and the Arabs give the fat itself first priority. It must be removed immediately, lest it take on the 'peculiar smell' of the elephant, and then boiled at a very high temperature.

It should then be strained, and, when tolerably cool, be poured into vessels, and secured. No salt is necessary, provided it is thoroughly boiled. When an animal is killed, the flesh should be properly dried, before boiling down, otherwise the fat will not melt thoroughly, as it will be combined with the water contained in the body. The fat should be separated as well as possible from the meat; it should then be hung in long strips upon a line and exposed in the sun to dry.

The final result is called 'reveet'. It is highly prized because it can be eaten on the march without bread, and it's 'extremely nourishing'. If a man is carrying dried meat instead, the 'best is that of the giraffe and hippopotamus'. Dried into strips, this meat is not eaten like jerky. Instead, it is pounded into 'coarse sawdust' and mixed into curry and rice.

The Arabs make a first-class dish of *melach*, by mixing a quantity of pounded dried meat with a thick porridge of *dhurra* [sorghum] meal, floating in a soup of *barmian* (waker) [aubergine, eggplant], with onions, salt, and red peppers; this is an admirable thing if the party is pressed for time.

As exotic as it may seem, elephant fat is straightforward on the symbolic plane, because it doesn't have one: it's eaten as a prosaic matter of survival. By contrast, the French custom of *menu droit* is entirely driven by symbolism. Translated literally, *menu droit* means 'small right'. It was a dish of the most prized bits taken from the downed stag at the conclusion of the royal hunt, and consisted of 'the muzzle, tongue, ears, testicles, *franc-boyau*, heart artery, and the little strings attached to the kidneys'. Following the ceremonial presentation of these parts, they were brought to the kitchen, cooked and served to

Result of a Morning's Hippopotamus Hunt on Mlembo River, Rhodesia, Africa,
c. 1910, photographic print on stereo card.

the royal couple. Tellingly, the word *franc-boyau* is so obscure
that no definitions appear in ancient or modern French dic-
tionaries. It may or may not have anything to do with *boyau*,
which refers to the intestines.

Not meat but still venison, this extraordinary dish left
no period recipes that I've been able to discover, and today
has morphed into a sort of ragout made of 'byproducts and
extremities (*issues et extremités*)', which is to say that it's become
hot dog soup. As the American manufacturers of 'pink slime'
(which they called 'lean finely te

xtured beef', or pulverized beef scraps) discovered, weird
food tastes better when it's got a wordy name. And even bet-

French Happiness

Isaac Cruikshank, *French Happiness, English Misery*, 1793, satirical print.
On the left, four ragged and starving sans-culottes fight over a frog, with
scenes of death in the background; on the right, in an English tavern, four
men overeat at a table laden with food, a fat dog lies on the floor and a cat
has caught a mouse.

ter if the words are French. The renaming trick has worked for sweetbreads, escargot and frog legs, to name just a few. Under the heading 'Frog' (*grenouille*), the *Larousse gastronomique* explains that frog legs are enjoyed across Europe, and are today commonly eaten in Germany, Italy and France. The British were unique in their refusal to eat them, but when Auguste Escoffier began cooking at the Carlton Hotel in London in the late 1890s, the legendary chef managed to coax the Prince of Wales to try them by calling them *cuisses de nymphes aurore* – legs of the dawn nymphs.

In sum, there is game, there is meat, and there is the stuff in between. It's the stuff in between that's troubling, for the human mind loathes ambiguities. In America frogs are governed by game laws, and to hunt them requires a small game hunting licence. But as with alligators, turtles, and reptiles and amphibians in general, their flesh might be 'fish' or 'meat'. In the southern state of Missouri, the difference depends on the method used to take them. As 'fish', a frog is fished using net, line, snares, grabbing or a gig (a sort of giant fork). As 'game', a frog is hunted using a small-calibre rifle, a pistol, a pellet gun or a bow. To hunt or fish for frogs requires different licences, and the food status of the frog is conditional on the method. If fished with a fishing licence, the frog is fish. If hunted with a hunting licence, it's meat. What the mouth tastes, and what the mind thinks, are truly two different things.

2

The Culinary Crucible: Of Law and Lusciousness

A fat swan loved he best of any roast.

Geoffrey Chaucer, *Canterbury Tales*, describing the Monk

Pope John XII (*c.* 937–964) remains infamous for his creative depravity. In addition to turning the Vatican into a whorehouse and having sex with his niece, blinding his confessor, castrating and killing a cardinal, raising his glass in toast to the Devil and indulging in just about every debauchery imaginable, he had the gall to go 'hunting publicly', complained a shocked Liudprand, bishop of Cremona (*c.* 922–972). John XII was pope during the *Saeculum obscurum*, the 'dark ages' of the papacy, but religious men have offended the public for centuries by overindulging in hunting. Not only did wealthy priests hunt with horses and dogs, emulating the trappings of nobles, but even monks grew fat dining on game-laden tables. Their continuing indulgence prompted Robert Burton to lambast Jesuit priests in his *Anatomy of Melancholy* (1621) for insisting that others eat sparingly, even as they 'play the gluttons themselves'.

In medieval Europe, the extensive hunting privileges of the clergy were cause for popular resentment. During the reign of Henry III of England, the Charter of the Forest outlined the

Detail of mural by Ezra Winter illustrating the characters in *The Canterbury Tales* by Geoffrey Chaucer. According to the inscription, the figures are (left to right): 'the Merchant, with his Flemish beaver hat and forked beard; the Friar; the Monk; the Franklin; the Wife of Bath; the Parson and his brother the Ploughman, riding side by side'.

king's will regarding the taking of game in his lands. Established in 1217, it extended protections to the common man against the abuses of the aristocracy. For example, it eliminated the practice of chopping off body parts from starving peasants caught poaching the king's deer.

> No one shall henceforth lose life or limb because of our venison, but if anyone has been arrested and convicted of taking venison he shall be fined heavily if he has the means; and if he has not the means, he shall lie in our prison for a year and a day.

Given that the previous penalty was either amputation of hands or hanging by the neck until dead, a year of jail time was a remarkable show of leniency. But the punishment was

still profound for the peasantry, for true game meat, or the 'venison' of the beasts of the chase, was explicitly classed as the food of the first and second estates (the nobility and the clergy), and off limits to the third (the peasantry). The next provision of the Charter of the Forest announced that 'any archbishop, bishop, earl or baron whatever who passes through our forest shall be allowed to take one or two beasts', but that limit was so routinely ignored that Guillaume Budé was prompted to quip in his *Traité de la vénerie* (1572): '*Non est inquirendum, unde venit venison*' (It is not to be inquired, whence comes the venison). Though kings periodically chastised the clergy, these warnings had no effect. Over centuries, noted Henry Charles Fitzroy Somerset, Duke of Beaufort, in *Hunting* (1885), 'the priest grew as mighty a hunter as the baron.'

Religious laws oddly reinforced the consumption of meat even as they advocated fasting. As a reflection of Catholic obser - vances, *A Propre New Booke of Cokery* (1545) divided up its menus into 'meat days' and 'fish days', with birds and mammals falling under the category of 'meat', and eggs and dairy falling

Marthe Picard (Ecoliers de Paris), 'Eat less meat to save our livestock', 1918.

under 'fish'. It began by providing the hunter with a schedule describing what kinds of meats in season at different times of year, and how they ought to be dressed and served at table:

> A Mallarde is good after a frost till candlemas so is a Tele
> [teal] and other wylde foule that Swymmeth. A Woodcoke
> is best from October to Lente and so is all other birdes as
> Dusels Thressels / Robins and suche other.

After a bowl of soup, a typical menu opened with a 'first service' of boiled meat, chickens with bacon, powdered beef (which had been boiled, then pulverized to fine, powder-like consistency), pies, a goose, a pig, roast beef, roast veal and custard, followed by roast lamb, roasted capons, roasted hares, chickens, peahens, bacon, venison and a tart. This was followed by a series of mutton pies, venison pasties (presumably of roe deer) and pasties of 'falow dere in a dishe', bringing the diner to the 'second service', which included a stunning array of game birds: ducks, pigeons, teals, gulls, curlews, bitterns, bustards, pheasants, woodcocks, quails, 'a disshe of larkes' and 'two pasties of red dere in a disshe'.

Larks continued to be consumed by French children singing 'Bonjour Guillaume' (Hello William), a happy song about a boy eating lark pâté, and they showed up on tables all the way to the nineteenth-century White House, which routinely served wild meats long before big-game-hunter Teddy Roosevelt's administration. Gulls, however, seem to have quickly fallen out of favour. The bird is an opportunistic eater that feasts on garbage, and complaints were often raised regarding the flavour of other fish-eating birds such as pelicans. Though the gull is perfectly edible, it probably tastes a lot like rotten seafood. Nonetheless, it did not appear on the 'fisshe daies' menu. For that, it had to be an egg.

Along with the strictures for fasting for Lent, much of the religious justification for declaring the beaver's tail, the capybara and the egg to be 'fish' came from Thomas Aquinas's *Summa Theologiae*, written between 1265 and 1278. 'In fasting, in chastity', 2 Corinthians 6 had stated, thus drawing a direct line from food to sexual desire. 'Wherefore', Aquinas stated, 'the Church forbade those who fast to partake of those foods which . . . afford most pleasure to the palate', because they incite the eater to lust. The most lust-inducing foods are 'the flesh of animals that take their rest on the earth, and of those that breathe the air and their products, such as milk from those that walk on the earth, and eggs from birds'. However, Aquinas explained, it is meats properly speaking – that is, the muscle flesh of mammals that 'are more like man in body' – that 'afford greater pleasure as food'. This pleasure directly contributes to sexual excess in men:

> From their consumption there results a greater surplus available for seminal matter, which when abundant becomes a great incentive to lust. Hence the Church has bidden those who fast to abstain especially from these foods.

Aquinas's argument for fasting traces itself back to man's exile from the Garden of Eden thanks to Eve and the snake, who are both to blame for tempting poor Adam into what Aquinas called '*concupiscentia*, which is the material principle of original sin'. It is concupiscence, or lusting after flesh, that is enabled when men eat mammals. It goes without saying that all the animals in Eden were asexual vegetarians. In Pieter Brueghel the Elder's engraving of Lust (*Luxuria*) from his series *The Seven Deadly Sins*, a feral rooster occupies the very centre of this anti-Eden. A pair of balls dangles over his head,

Engraving after Pieter Brueghel the Elder, 'Luxuria' (Lust), 1558, from
The Seven Deadly Sins, or *The Seven Vices*.

making the male genitals ('cock and balls') the touchstone of
this world. But the ceremonial figure presiding over the festi-
vities is a stag with a ball or apple stuffed in its mouth in the
manner of a suckling pig, and his body becomes the shelter
and sustenance for the monstrous coupling taking place inside
the primitive teepee made from its skin.

Thus meat, and especially game meat, was said to incite
sex and other 'animal' activities. Some of the earliest examples
of printed pornography took full advantage of the association by lewdly exposing naked ladies waggling the plumage
of wild birds from indiscreet orifices, and illustrating 'deer
parks' that were, rather, stables of bendy mistresses. By contrast, public-minded satirical images hid the Devil in the details.
For example, in one caricature by James Gillray, a buxom
kitchen maid hurries past a book called *Doe Hunting, an Ode by
an Old Buck Hound*, even as she's being chased by the horny

James Gillray, *Sandwich! Carrots!*, 1796, satirical print. A girl pushes a wheelbarrow of carrots along Bond Street, looking over her shoulder at an older man, possibly the son of John Montagu, 4th Earl of Sandwich, who tugs at her apron. The bookshop in the background displays the titles *A Chip off the Old Block*; *Doe Hunting an Ode by an Old Buck Hound*; *A List of Servant Maids*; *The Beauties of Bond Street*; and *A Journey through Life – from Maddox Street unto Conduit Street & Back Again.*

son of the Earl of Sandwich. Illiterate or inattentive viewers, including children and the lower classes in general, would miss the reference entirely. These same groups didn't participate in the aristocratic sport of hunting.

Confusingly, it is God himself who 'inspires people to like to roast meat', noted the anonymous author of a thirteenth-century Andalusian cookbook:

> He inspires the cooking and making of it with whatever will improve and augment its strength, flavour, and char-acteristic virtue so it may be cause to improve the opposing natures of the people, for there are people of sanguine, phlegmatic, choleric and melancholic humour; some cook with water and salt and find it good, others cook with vinegar, others with milk and others with sumac and *murri* and so on.

This cookbook accepted meat as a 'virtue', for the theory of the humours was also a theory of food, operating under the notion that a surfeit of one humour, such as phlegm, should be balanced by eating a food with its opposite properties. This thinking persists today in the talismanic properties assigned to aphrodisiacs. Notably, the theory of the humours also appears in Aquinas's argument regarding the need to abstain from meat, which tends to encourage lustful thoughts, along with the 'act of procreation'.

Aquinas conceded that wine and vegetables make the eater 'flatulent'. Unlike lust, however, farting wasn't a sin; it was only the overproduction of seminal fluid that preoccupied him. His legacy helps explain why the quintessential 'date night' meal remains crusty bread and a good cut of steak. However, the moral arguments for and against game meat are older than Christianity. 'I do not know why Homer has not described hunting as a glory to man and as ennobling those that pursue it', complained Synesius of Cyrene (373–414 CE). He 'makes us poor men [seem] shameless and utterly vile', even as refined men 'shiver at the sight of wild beasts' flesh fresh from the fire'. Instead of game, what do they eat? 'They seek the lightest wine, the thickest honey, the thinnest olive oil, and the heaviest wheat.'

For every ancient philosopher that praised hunting for its moral benefits, another denounced game meat as a sure path

Vision of St Eustace, from the Trinity Altar, Wawel Cathedral, Krakow, Poland, 1467.

to disease. 'They say moreover that the consumption of meat compromises our health', commented Porphyry of Tyre (234–*c.* 305 CE) on the Epicureans. 'It is recovered by a light diet and abstinence from meat, and is therefore preserved by the same means.' According to his way of thinking, vegetarianism is also a sign of social and intellectual superiority, for the masses cannot be convinced to stay away from meat. 'They are persuaded that all the pleasures which are in motion and gratifying are healthy, the pleasures of love included', Porphyry complained. These 'are never good for anything, and often very harmful'.

Even as game meat was cast as a status symbol that was simultaneously naughty and healthful, so too was hunting itself described in radically alternating terms. Apologists cast hunting as a moral occupation that prevented knights from the sin of sloth, but a great deal of ritual hunting, the kind practised by aristocrats and kings, was undertaken strictly for love of the chase. In the *Libre qui es de l'ordre de cavalleria* (*The Book of the Order of Chivalry*), written between 1279 and 1283, Majorcan mystic Ramon Llull framed it in terms of the military arts. 'Knyghtes ougt to hunte at hertes, at bores and other wyld bestes, for in doynge these thynges the knyghtes exercyse them to armes.' The royal hunt was its own justification, affirming an entitled position that would significantly strengthen over the next few centuries as it sublimated the pageantry of war. By the sixteenth century, Guillaume Budé announced that the king hunts 'not to provision the kitchen but to draw from it the pleasure and benefits of physical exercise'. Inside a framework where the hunt rehearsed the terms and tactics of war, the stag was not eaten for the same reason that the body of a warrior fallen in battle was not eaten. To do so would replicate the terms of cannibalism.

Lucas Cranach the Elder, *Stag Hunt of Frederick III, Elector of Saxony*, 1529.

Within the Christian tradition the stag also invoked the Eucharist. For example, the name of the great hall in *Beowulf* is 'Heorot', which means 'hall of the hart', and this 'hart strong in his antlers' was understood to refer to the human soul. Before his conversion to Christianity, St Eustace was a Roman soldier named Placidus. As described in the *Golden Legend* (1275),

> So on a day, as he was on hunting, he found a herd of harts, among whom he saw one more fair and greater than the other . . . And [the hart] spake to him, saying: Placidus, wherefore followest me hither? I am appeared to thee in this beast for the grace of thee. I am Jesu Christ.

Through such saints and Old Testament figures such as Jacob, blessed by his father Isaac for bringing him venison, the Holy Hunter came into being, strengthening the clergy's claim to special privileges to the king's forest.

However, the model knight wasn't a saint, but Tristram (or Tristan) of Arthurian legend, who defined the ritual hunt and represented the epitome of refinement in the sport. To those who would 'learn the art of venery', wrote George Turbervile in 1576, 'let him give eare, to skilfull Trystrams lore'. In one thirteenth-century version of the legend, written by Gottfried von Strassburg, the boy Tristram is a kidnapped castaway in the land of Cornwall, where he runs into a hunting party coursing a stag. He watches as the Master of the Hunt brings it down, and then stretches out the carcass 'by all four legs, like a pig'. The hunter plans to skin the quarry, then cut it into four equal parts, first by slicing it in half down the spine, then slicing it across. Horrified by this treatment of the carcass, Tristram stops him, and insists there's a better way to 'break' the stag. Gottfried proceeds to devote such attention to the dressing of the carcass that it required a full chapter and half to describe it, but these passages would disappear from sub-sequent versions of the legend, which morphed into a tragic love story. Along with prudishness, the rising neuroses of modernity banished the bloody carcass from the literature of romance and chivalry.

By the advent of the Industrial Age, the most refined cuisine came to occupy that precise space between 'dying of hunger' and eating away 'the future', noted Alexandre Balthazar Laurent Grimod de la Reynière, dancing nimbly between the two poles of savagery and seduction. For those who would practise the art of living well, he imposed the 'Code Gour-mand', a set of rules that were highly demanding because of the human tendency to excess. To posterity, his *Almanach des gourmands* (1807), left the impossible 'Roast of Roasts' (*Rôti sans pareil*), a recipe that is best understood as an epic novel dis-guised as a nursery rhyme. I have paraphrased the rather long instructions here:

> Begin with a 'pretty' olive stuffed with capers and
> anchovies.
> Stuff the olive into a warbler from which the head and
> feet [and feathers] have been removed.
> Truss the warbler and stuff it inside a 'fat' ortolan.
> Stuff the whole ortolan into a lark from which the head,
> feet, and bones have been removed.
> Lard the lark and stuff it inside a deboned thrush.
> > [From this point on it seems to be assumed that
> > each bird will be plucked, fully dressed, and
> > deboned.]
> Truss the thrush and stuff it into a quail, preferably a
> domestic quail.
> Wrap the quail in a grape leaf and stuff it into a lapwing.

THE PUCK PRESS

Keppler

THE REVIVAL

Udo Keppler, *The Revival of an Ancient Skin Game*, 1912. This is a political take on the Bible story of Jacob and Esau. On the far left Jacob presents Isaac with a steaming dish of venison labelled 'Savory Politics', while Esau approaches on the right with a deer over his shoulders labelled 'Popularity'.

Cape the lapwing lightly and stuff it into a golden
    plover.

Bard the plover and stuff it inside a partridge, by
    preference a red partridge.

Stuff the partridge inside a young woodcock, with flesh
    as 'succulent' and 'tender' as that of Mlle Volnais.

Roll it in breadcrumbs and stuff it inside a teal.

Bard the teal and stuff it inside a guinea fowl.

Bard the guinea fowl and stuff it inside a young duck,
    preferably wild.

Stuff the young duck into a spayed virgin female
    chicken, as 'white as Mme Belmont, as well fleshed
    as Mlle De Vienne, plump as Mlle L. Contat'.

Stuff this chicken into a young pheasant that, above all
    else, has been properly hung (*bien mortifié*).

Stuff the pheasant into a fat, well-aged wild goose.

Stuff this 'young and pretty goose' into a 'very beautiful'
    turkey, as 'white and plump as Mlle Arsène'.

Finally, place this bird inside a 'beautiful' bustard, and fill
    up any empty spaces with chestnuts, sausages or
    other forms of stuffing.

Cook for 24 hours in a low fire, and serve.

Reynière was quick to confess that he did not invent this
dish. It came from ancient Rome to eighteenth-century
French tables by way of a ribald tale, 'Galanterie d'un boucher
à sa maîtresse' (The Gallantry of a Butcher to His Mistress),
a version of which was performed in Paris in 1733, along with
the *Ballet des dindons* (Turkey Ballet). For Reynière, this exceptional roast captured the 'quintessence of the plains, the
forests, the wetlands, and the best of the kitchen courtyard',
and for the same reason, this recipe is not prescriptive. The
cook is free to vary the birds according to the seasons, the

Canadian-American actress and opera singer Christie MacDonald wearing artificial birds on her hat and the bodice of her dress, 1902.

location and the budget. Due to the varied locations and timing of the hunts required to obtain these birds, some of which are now endangered, this dish is exceptionally diffi-cult to prepare. The idea of this roast is also vaguely funny because of its food-chain literalism, even as it enacts the theo-logically informed idea of dominion. Specifically, it dramatizes nature's abundance of cooperative flesh, including the flesh of 'young and pretty' women as luscious as these wild birds within birds. There are sixteen birds in this recipe, and only three – the turkey, the chicken and the quail – are domestic by preference. The rest are game birds, waiting to be chased, and all the more desirable because of it.

The brilliance of this recipe, Reynière concluded, is the idea of placing 'one animal into another', starting with the tiny warbler and ending with the bustard. But he neglected to mention the final animal being stuffed: the wealthy bastard at the table, waiting to be served.

3

It Tastes Like Chicken: Falconry, Trapping and Subsistence Hunting

Among quadrupeds, the hare is the finest [game].

Martial (40–*c.* 104 CE)

When Jacques-Auguste de Thou was invited to dine with the Count of Gévaudan in 1589, he was surprised to see that every plate of small game and wild birds arrived at the table missing 'its head, or a wing, or a thigh, or some other part'. The count explained that it was on account of the eagles. To feed their young, they picked off capons, chickens, ducks and other domesticated birds that roamed in kitchen courtyards, and would even carry off lambs, kids and piglets. But the eagles' best hunting grounds were out in the country, where they would take 'pheasants, partridge, hazel grouse, wild ducks, hare and roe deer'. As soon as the parent birds dropped off their catch and flew off to resume hunting, waiting shepherds would steal the carcass from the chicks. Often, however, they were not quick enough. By the time they had snatched the meat away, eaglets had already managed to gnaw off a limb. This was the reason the small game was 'mutilated' before arriving at the table.

'The Docile Falcon', 19th-century print.

The shepherds in Thou's story would presumably give the eaglets to the count, who would them train them in falconry. The Polish legend of Lech and Gniezno tells of the first Duke of Poland, a nobleman named Lech, who attempts to capture a white eagle for this purpose. In this instance, however, the eagle fights back to protect her brood, and in recognition of her bravery, she becomes the emblem of Poland, and its first capital is named Gniezno, which according to the legend means 'nest'.

A Kazakh proverb declares: 'There are three things a real man should have: a fast horse, a hound, and a golden eagle.' In Central Asia, the tradition of hunting with golden eagles dates back to the Mongolian conquest of the twelfth century, and Kazakhstan remains one of the few places where hunting with eagles is still practised today. Kazakh men who train eagles are known as *berkutchi*, and disdain hunting with falcons as the sport of women and children. Within falconry the symbolic value assigned to each bird is consistent across many cultures, with the eagle consistently occupying the top rung. For example, according to the *Boke of St Albans* (1486), the emperor hunts with the eagle. The king sits directly beneath the emperor in rank, and hunts with the 'Ger falcon' or gyrfalcon (*Falco rusticolus*), the largest member of the falcon group. Below dukes and barons, the lady hunts with the 'Marlyon' or merlin (*F. columbarius*), a small falcon commonly known as the 'pigeon hawk'. Such ladies would have included the author of the *Boke*

'Manfred Seated and Pointing to Two Kneeling Men with Falcons', in *De arte venandi cum avibus* (1596).

of St Albans, which is credited to Juliana Berners, the prioress of Sopwell nunnery. Beneath the lady in rank, the yeoman hunts with the goshawk. At the bottom of the hierarchy, the knave hunts with a kestrel.

As much descriptive of the symbolic order as it was of a social hierarchy, the list indicated a very specific range of predatory birds, each of which represented a different set of prey and hunting habits. The medieval insistence on distinguishing 'falconry' from 'hawking', which today strikes the ear as being fussy, reflected the fact that falcons (Falconidae), being long-wing birds, are not hawks (Accipitridae), which are short-wing. To confuse them was as absurd as mistaking eagles for owls, which are both broad-wings. They were flown for 'eagling' and 'owling' respectively. Long known as the sport of kings, falconry often involved hundreds of birds because each kind took particular game.

Interestingly, the bird's hunting habits also varied by its sex. Male falcons, for example, took partridges and quail, whereas the female falcons took herons and cranes. It is for this reason that the *Boke of St Albans* indicated that kings hunt with 'the Ger falcon and the Tercel of the Ger falcon', just as princes hunted with the 'falcon Gentle [the peregrine] and the Tercel gentle'. The term 'tercel' or 'tiercel' refers to the male, which is always smaller than the female falcon of his species. In falconry, in other words, the default bird is female.

Both peregrines and gyrfalcons hunt other birds. In *Birds of India: Being a Natural History of All the Birds Known to Inhabit Continental India* (1864), for example, T. C. Jerdon, Surgeon Major of the Madras Army, noted that the houbara bustard was 'much hawked both in the Punjab and Sindh', but the bird exclusively used for this purpose was not a hawk but a falcon known as *charragh*, the saker falcon (*F. sacer*). According to Jerdon, the Indian houbara was chased as a pest species and not hunted as food, even though its flesh was 'exceedingly tender'. When falconry was expressly practised for culinary reasons, it was the yeoman's bird, the goshawk, that was flown. This bird was known as the 'cook's hawk' because of its spectacular hunting skills and its predilection for taking hares, rabbits, grouse and other game that directly contributed to the table. Game taken in this fashion, Thou had observed, was believed to have 'a taste above all that's sold at market'. This assessment was seconded by the *Propre Booke of Cokery*, which pointed out: 'Fesauntes Partriche and Raill be ever good but best when thei bee taken with a Hauke.' By contrast, the knave's bird, the kestrel, primarily hunted mice, lizards and insects. The kestrel was thus useless for food. If servants indeed trained one (and most likely they did not), it would have been seen as a risible affectation of the sport most closely associated with knighthood.

Historically, falconry invoked a certain set of ideals regarding the conduct of those of noble rank, particularly among the male nobles of Europe and the samurai in Japan. The earliest evidence of falconry is found in Khorsabad in the palace of Sargon II, who reigned in Assyria *c.* 722–705 BCE. In the first-century epic poem the *Shahnameh* (or *Shah-nama*, Book of Kings, 977–1010 CE) by the Persian poet Ferdowsi, the prince Tahmuras domesticates wild animals, tames predators and invents the sport of falconry:

> Among the well-armed birds he chose the hawk
> And noble falcon, and began to tame them
> While men looked on amazed. His orders were
> To rear the birds and speak to them with kindness.

The reality of falconry was more prosaic. The excesses of falconry enthusiasts such as the tenth-century king of Germany

Henry I, known as 'The Fowler', because he paid more attention to his birds than to his subjects, eventually led to the sport being associated with the moral dissolution of the wealthy. In 'The Knight's Tale', for example, Chaucer noted that knights attending a feast displayed their hunting birds and dogs in the dining hall as pure status symbols, so that guests could gossip about 'what hawks sit on the perch above / What hounds lie on the floor below'. The elaborate rituals associated with falconry explain why popular resentments fixated on the pampered bird itself. Highly expensive to own and maintained in great luxury, trained falcons might wear hoods ornamented with pearls, and rings of pure gold around their legs. Functioning much like dog collars today, these rings made it possible to identify the bird's owner if it failed to return. A thief who stole a falcon would be punished in a curious way: the falcon would be allowed to eat 6 ounces (170 grams) of the flesh from the living thief's breast, unless he could pay a stiff fine to the owner and another to the king.

The sadistic punishment parodied the process of training the birds to obey humans. Usually, they were caught young, hooded and placed in a cage, and hand-fed at regular intervals by the falconer. In some cases they were trained to respond to a whistle; in others they imprinted on the sound of their keeper's voice and would only respond to the human who raised them. As the birds grew older, they were fastened to a string by one leg, allowed to fly a short distance, then called back and greeted with a bit of meat. To train them to hunt hares, the falconer stuffed a hare with a live chicken and dragged it along. If the falcon was successful, it would be rewarded with the chicken's head and the liver. A bit of chicken was also the reward when the falcons were trained to hunt birds such as kites, herons and cranes.

Kitagawa Utamaro, *First Dream: Mount Fuji, Hawks and Aubergines,*
1798–1801.

As far as falcons were concerned, all game birds tasted like chicken. Amusingly, humans tend to agree. According to Bob Bennett, the author of *Storey's Guide to Raising Rabbits* (2009), most people say that 'snake, frogs' legs, pheasant, alligator, iguana, turtle, mako shark, and nutria' taste like chicken. Apparently, so do mouse deer and capybaras. As Fergus 'the Forager' Drennan noted in an article in *The Guardian* in 2007, 'the classic descriptive cliché for practically any previously untried meat is that it either tastes like chicken or, more curiously, tuna.' He disagrees. In his opinion:

> Badger tastes somewhat beefy, fox a lot like mountain goat, squirrel like a turkey-lamb chimera, seagull like a rich ducky pheasant with a whisker of cat, and mole like rabbit with a hint of liver.

Bedouin men on horseback with falcons, early 20th century.

But old habits die hard. As Minnie C. Fox's succinct Kentucky recipe for broiled squirrel in *The Blue Grass Cookbook* (1904) instructs: 'If young and tender, broil as you would chicken. If old, bake as you would chicken.'

Wild rabbits don't taste like domesticated rabbits; wild turkey doesn't taste like domesticated turkey; and farm-raised ostrich doesn't taste like an overgrown chicken. It looks and tastes like dry beef. These inconsistencies reveal the dominance of ideation over taste, for we eat with our eyes and taste with our brains. This potent interplay was the subject of a Northern Baroque painting by Jan Brueghel the Elder and Peter Paul Rubens. A visual feast, *Allegory of Taste* (1618) foregrounds a wealth of traditional European small game. Young peacocks, peahens, swans and braces of songbirds skewered on sticks appear, as do hares, rabbits and deer. It is notable that cows, calves, sheep and 'fat pigges' make no appearance in this painting, perhaps because beef, bacon, veal, mutton and pork can be eaten year-round, says the *Propre New Booke of Cokery*, with a slight air of boredom. But the *Allegory of Taste* is also an allegory of time, as game animals are not at their peak at the same time of the year, with the 'barren doe', for example, being best in winter. She is shown gutted and hanging in the background of the painting, next to a deer park full of semi-domesticated stags.

In the foreground of the *Allegory of Taste*, a hare lounges across the day's take of game. Is she a good choice for supper? 'If the cleft in her lip spread much, is wide and ragged', Amelia Simmons instructs ladies out snaring their suppers, 'she is old'. If someone else other than the cook has been out hunting for game, she also needs to know how long the animal has been lying around, especially if it has not been properly dressed in the field. 'Hares, are white flesh'd and flexible when new and fresh kill'd', Simmons tells her readers in *American*

Jan Brueghel the Elder and Peter Paul Rubens, *Allegory of Taste*, 1618.

Cookery; or, the Art of Dressing Viands, Fish, Poultry and Vegetables
(1796). 'If stale, their flesh will have a blackish hue, like old
pigeons.' These considerations are important when buying
food in a marketplace instead of a supermarket where food is
labelled. In the absence of a standardized system, each cook

had to be an amateur naturalist if she wanted to ensure she wasn't being fooled.

To assist her readers, Simmons discussed the best way for the home cook to assess the freshness of duck, woodcock, snipe, partridge, pigeon, blackbird, thrush, lark and 'wild fowl in general', as well as hare, leveret and rabbit. Of rabbits, she commented, the 'wild are the best'. They were also everyday table fare, which is why so many eighteenth-century cats were being fobbed off as rabbits in the first place. The birds and mammals that Simmons recommended were chiefly wild, with only the duck, pigeon and rabbit being understood to come in handy, domesticated versions as well. But the most important detail that every home cook should know was the sex of the animal she is preparing to behead.

> The female in almost every instance is preferable to the male, and particularly so in the Peacock, which, tho' beautifully plumaged, is tough, hard, stringy, and untasted, even indelicious – while the Pea Hen is exactly otherwise, the queen of all birds.

That passage is worth repeating simply for the word 'indelicious', though it is also a useful reminder that peacocks used to be regarded as colourful turkeys. By the end of the eighteenth century, the peacock was ornamenting pioneer tables and not just being served to royalty. In the estimation of gourmands, 'a platter of peacock occupies the first rank', wrote Apicius, 'provided they be dressed in such a manner that the hard and tough parts be tender'. The second most desirable dishes, he continued, are 'dishes made of rabbit'.

The question of flavour versus expectation plays out strongly when the subject is small game, since such creatures were conventionally trapped or snared rather than hunted. Many of these species were small, plentiful and destructive. There was nothing 'noble' about the killing of pests. From a symbolic perspective, the meat that results from falconry is different from that yielded by trapping, as each of these terms reflects different cultural relations between the hunter and the hunted. When trapped, a hare is vermin. When hunted, it's delicious.

François Fortin's *Innocent Tricks (Les Ruses innocentes*, 1660) is not a manual of falconry, the hunt or venery, because these practices were privileges of the aristocracy. Instead, Fortin focused on 'tricks' used by peasants to catch small pest species, which included ortolans, blackbirds, migratory ducks, herons, rabbits, fish and the occasional 'stinking beast', meaning foxes, badgers and weasels. So that the lord who owned the farmland would know what the peasants were up to, Fortin chronicled the various ruses they used to fool and capture their prey, such as dressing up as cows or disguising themselves as bushes. Precursors to modern camouflage suits, these costumes were effective. But sneaking up on a rabbit while draped in the hide of a farm animal? This is not hunting. It's a farce with booby traps. There is no sport in the peasant's actions, merely a supper of sparrows.

My father, who grew up in Korea under Japanese occupation, remembers that hunters were required to store their rifles in the police station. During hunting season, they had permission to retrieve their arms, and the schoolchildren would be sent out with pots and pans. Their job was to make the kind of racket at which little kids excel in order to drive wild boars high into the hills, where the hunters were waiting for them. He recalls these drives as a fun game. But the purpose was to control a highly dangerous pest animal; there wasn't a feast to celebrate. In *Sketches of Indian Field Sports* (1827), Daniel Johnson, a surgeon in the East India Company, describes a class of lower-caste Hindus called 'Shekarees', who make their living by 'catching birds, hares, and other animals'. Using pole-nets, camouflage traps and other tricks, they would catch partridges, wild peacocks and 'jungle fowl' (the wild parent of domesticated chickens). The parrots and pigeons would be sold at market to 'Mahometans, and a few to the low casts of Hindoos', for up to a penny each. 'These people eat them for

Martinet, *The Cook*, c. 1780. A rabbit hangs from the chopping block.

food', Johnson added in surprise. His reaction had less to do with the food quality of the birds, which were elsewhere considered to be delicacies, than the classed status of the method by which they were taken, designating their deaths as exterminations and their bodies as unfit food for humans.

Due to their diminutive size, birds captured in nets require a great deal of effort to prepare for the table. Thus the French (possibly French-Canadian) children's song 'Alouette' is an upbeat ditty about plucking larks, a tedious chore assigned to small hands. Each stanza of the song goes through a different body part: I'll pluck your beak, your head, your eyes, your back, your wings, your belly and so on, following a sequence which also walks the plucker through this necessary step in game bird food preparation. Whether such a supper seems depressing or delightful typically boils down to class snobbery versus economic need, for the smallest of small game occupies the social extremes. In traditional Polish cuisine, for example, the unusual abundance of game recipes reflects the 'princely wealth of the wealthy', noted Jean Karsavina, 'but also the poverty of the poor'. During the Middle Ages, Polish princesses feasted on sumptuous dishes such as 'Hungarian-style Spit Roasted Shoulder of Venison', the recipe for which was recovered by food historian Maria Dembinska. To 'great fanfare', Dembinska imagines, the venison would be carried in to the great hall on a spit, and presented for carving. By contrast, destitute

Jacques Le Moyne de Morgues, 'Florida Indians, Disguised under Deerskins, Hunting Deer', from *Der ander Theil, der newlich erfundenen Landschafft Americae* (1603).

Poles would go into the forest and catch small game for dinner. These recipes don't appear in Dembinska's book, because they typically weren't recorded.

The closest approximation to a Polish peasant game dish is *bigos* ('hunter's stew'), which is the national dish of Poland. Interestingly, it unites both privilege and poverty, and there is a great deal of variation among versions. A stew of various meats and cabbage, the dish became famous through the writings of Adam Mickiewicz, whose epic poem *Pan Tadeusz* (1834) was translated into prose English by Marcel Weyland as *The Last Foray in Lithuania*. To celebrate the end of a dramatic bear hunt, the hunters bring out the *bigos*, a stew of cabbage, sauerkraut and braised meats that they brought to the forest with them. Mickiewicz wrote:

> Pickled cabbage comes foremost, and properly chopped,
> Which itself, is the saying, will in one's mouth hop;
> In the boiler enclosed, with its moist bosom shields
> Choicest morsels of meat raised on greenest of fields.

The meat that gets stewed isn't necessarily game, and it wasn't from the day's hunt, because it takes days of slow cooking for the flavours to blend. The bear killed at the end of Mickiewicz's hunt, for example, did not get added to the pot. 'While it is true that *bigos* is a hunter's stew', wrote art historian Anja Bryszki in an email to me, 'it was also a staple when I was growing up because it requires small amounts of various meat scraps and hence was extremely compatible with food/meat shortages that plagued Poland since 1945.' She noted that in the late 1950s, or the immediate post-Stalinist period, the Communist version of *bigos* was made entirely with cuts of domesticated meat. The recipe Olga Robak's Polish grandmother uses is a combination of beef and pork; no venison or game birds. These variations in *bigos* underscore a human relationship to wildness that is always in flux, and what goes in the pot is frequently representative of individual rights and freedoms. The loss of hunting privileges has repeatedly served as sign of political oppression as well as economic disparity, for wealthy foreigners could buy permits to hunt Poland's ex‑ceptional forests. Since then, *bigos* has become 'a popular way for making do', Bryszki notes, and 'every cook has her own version' – even vegetarians.

Game on the Run

There is big game, and there is small game. There is legal hunting, and there is poaching. The law tends to look away when the poaching extends to small game, because squirrels, raccoons and their ilk are frequently aligned with vermin, which have little value inside an economic system. Because of widespread poaching of wildlife, however, legal hunting in South America is restricted, as its natural ecologies have been severely impacted by it. There is no legal hunting in Brazil. Argentina, by contrast, is one of the few South American countries that support it, but it is largely restricted to the wing shooting of doves and pigeons, because these birds number in the millions and are serious agricultural pests. Foreigners legally hunt these birds for sport. Locals illegally hunt monkeys as food.

In 2007 *Spiegel Online* reported that the consumption of monkeys in Central and South America had increased so drastically that it posed a dire threat to the survival of primate populations. Because it violates so many legal and cultural taboos, this kind of wild animal consumption has become its own food category, called 'bushmeat'. Distinct from game meat, it it typically implicates large animals that are geographically confined to certain areas – that is, 'the bush' – and which are also endangered due to human activities. Unlike poachers, who wilfully violate laws that regulate wild animals as property, bushmeat hunters begin with the assumption that wild animals belong to nature, like the air, hence the laws are invalid. In other words, game meat inhabits a set of rituals where even illegal deaths serve to reinforce the underlying social order. By contrast, bushmeat roughly exposes its fictions.

Among other things, a dietary reliance on bushmeat shows that the terms of hunting revise when the land is under siege. In times of war, the organizational terms of hunting disappear. 'There is not much game around here', complained a hungry Yankee soldier foraging in Tennessee near the end of the American Civil War. There was only '*Bear, Swamp Oppossom, Turkey, Tame pheasant* & Squirles & so forth . . . we don't grumble but try to eat them'. The everyday life of 'Billy Yank' during the American Civil War was marked by hunger and boredom relieved periodically by hunting. The same critters that disappointed hungry Northern Yankees were comfort food to 'Johnny Reb' from the South, where squirrels and opossums were staples of the local cuisine. As Bell Irvin Wiley related in *The Life of Johnny Reb: The Common Soldier of the Confederacy* (1943), one Rebel soldier from the Southern state of Virginia wrote:

> Yesterday a covey of partridges was flushed in the Field where we camped, they grew bewildered & squatted about in the field; three or four were caught. I caught one plump & full grown; yes and eat him too, picking his bones clean.

They could hunt all the game they wanted, but Yankee and Rebel soldiers were forbidden to plunder, meaning that it was

A Possum Hunt: The Possum Viewing his Finish, 1901. An African American man sitting on a branch reaches towards an opossum that has climbed to the top of the tree.

against military rules for soldiers to eat livestock belonging to civilians. Nonetheless, this rule was frequently broken, with Unionists telling tales of suicidal ducks and despondent chickens sacrificing themselves to the Cause. Local Southerners were also in the habit of letting their livestock pigs forage for acorns in the woods. Jokingly, Yankee soldiers would call the pigs 'slow deer', and shoot them for dinner.

Rebel soldiers were far less well provisioned than the Yankee troops, and they were often desperate for fresh protein. In the state of Florida, Rebels tried alligator meat, which 'tasted like catfish', reported one young soldier from Georgia. A Texan soldier took a liking to armadillo, the meat of which was 'far superior to any possum I ever eat [sic]'. (According to Diana Kennedy, the 'Julia Child of Mexico', armadillo is a traditional ingredient in tamales prepared by the Amuzgos of Oaxaca, Mexico.) These first-person accounts also illustrate the potent mixture of cultural, legal and political forces that inform hunting for game in the modern world. For soldiers fighting a terrible war, catching enough sparrows for a pie was cause to rejoice, and hunting was a happy diversion for both sides. A rabbit zooming through camp was an excuse to run after one's dinner, redefining 'game' animals as the object of purpose-driven playing.

As it happened, Rebel soldiers were nabbing many of the same creatures that sustained West Africans brought to the American South as slaves. The historian William Piersen noted

Theodore de Bry, after Jacques Le Moyne de Morgues, *Killing Alligators*, 1591.

that slaves had been more 'adventurous than European-Americans' in their willingness to eat opossum and raccoon, because game had traditionally supplemented their otherwise vegetarian diets in West Africa (as distinct from the meat-heavy diets of North Africa). Though there were exceptions, Southern slave owners generally didn't allow slaves to own firearms for hunting, but they could use dogs or traps, or catch game with their hands, and some were allowed to keep a small kitchen garden before and after the North won the American Civil War. During the Great Depression, gaunt children caught rabbits with their bare hands, a harsh social reality that puts the idea of wild animals as 'game' into a different perspective. The current, widespread perception of hunting as being cruel partly results from the 'Bugs Bunny' effect, which held up adorably anthropomorphized rabbits on one side and imposed classed and racist views on the other.

In reality, for many around the world, the ability to catch dinner still represents the difference between survival and starvation. Throwing rocks at rabbits falls out of the usual purview of hunting, for the value of game meat is not intrinsic to its quality or even taste, but reflects the rituals (or lack thereof) practised in its taking. Game is correctly 'game' when the animal is taken for sport or leisure. When those terms are evacuated, hunting becomes an exercise in vulnerability. 'They are welcome, then, to all deer and ostriches which they can catch', noted a reluctant young hunter in Charles Kingley's *Hypatia* (1853), set in fifth-century Alexandria. 'But I am not only penniless, but reduced myself to live, like the Laestrygons, on meat and nothing else; all crops and stocks for miles round being either burnt or carried off.' Without the ritualistic aspects of the hunt, there is merely the terrifying reality of hunger.

This aspect of hunting is often lost among the pleasant distractions of nostalgia trips. In a hunting expedition of 1902 in the Salmon River Breaks near Dixie, Idaho, American hunter John Danforth ate elk ribs for his lunch, and then encountered a herd of four black-tailed bucks and three does. He and his friend shot the largest male at 75 yards with a .30-30 Winchester, and then field dressed the buck, brought it back to camp, chopped firewood and 'roasted the marrow bones for supper'. Ribs and marrow still appear on middle-class menus, and the idea of eating them during a hunting trip feeds a satisfying narrative of frontier self-sufficiency. But the exigencies of a sustained wilderness trek can truly test one's intestinal fortitude as well as the gastronomic imagination. Samuel Hearne's famous *Journey from Prince of Wales's Fort in Hudson's Bay to the Northern Ocean in the Years 1769, 1770, 1771, and 1772*, first published in 1795, is as much a document of food practices among Native American tribes as it is of geographic exploration. Travelling with help of the Chippewa tribe, the representatives of the Hudson's Bay Company hunted as they moved across the land, sometimes going without food for days, gratefully taking partridges and rabbits when they could. When they lucked into a herd of larger game such as deer, they ate the entire animal, including the stomach with its grassy contents. But the delicacy that surpassed them all was the unborn fawn, beaver or buffalo calf removed from its mother's womb. 'I am not the only European who heartily joins in pronouncing them the greatest dainties that can be eaten', Hearne noted confidently. If the reader overcomes his 'prejudices' and tries one of these treats, Hearne declared, he will be immediately and 'excessively fond of them'.

Then the Natives ate the uterus. For Hearne, this crossed a gastronomic line, but he was honest enough to recognize that his revulsion was arbitrary. This delicacy was reserved for men and boys, as was the privilege of eating the penises. The latter was apt to be tough, Hearne observed, but was never to be

John C. Grabill, *Hunting Deer*, 1888.

cut with a knife, only torn with the teeth, with only the most rubbery mouthfuls thrown into the fire. It was considered bad luck for a woman to eat any sex parts. To Hearne's surprise, Native American men and some members of the Company were 'remarkably fond' of the emptied womb, which was 'well enough' if taken from does and beavers, he averred. But the 'moose and buffalo is very rank, and truly disgusting'. To prepare the uterus, the Chippewa removed it whole and held it over a smoky fire, then cut it into large slices that were boiled very briefly. The lining was studded with large nodes that resembled egg yolks, which the Chippewa 'eagerly devoured'.

Though this dish strained his palate, Hearne must have tried it repeatedly to be able to comment first-hand on the differences in its taste. By contrast, he found buffalo tripe to be 'exceedingly good', and prepared in a fashion that was far superior to the European method of boiling it for hours. He also conceded that the lesser stomachs of the buffalo, moose and deer weren't bad at all, though moose tended to be bitter. They were eaten raw, he commented, as were the kidneys of moose and buffalo, as practised by southern Native Americans:

> No sooner is one of those beasts killed, than the hunter rips up its belly, thrusts in his arm, snatches out the kidneys, and eats them warm, before the animal is quite dead. They also at times put their mouths to the wound the ball has made, and suck the blood, which they say quenches thirst, and is very nourishing.

Divested of the usual romantic haze, Hearne's culinary assessments throughout the *Journey* reflect an unusual degree of specificity. Moose, deer, elk, wapiti and other members of the cervid (deer) family retain unique flavour profiles across the entire spectrum of the body. All the better if the part is tasty, Hearne thought, but still edible if not, reflecting the roaring appetite of a young man with an adventuresome spirit. Much like game recipes prior to the nineteenth century, these explorers consistently underscored the importance of consuming the entire animal, for when the game is truly wild, its availability is unpredictable, and all food was essential when on the trail. Compared to the stringent demands of subsistence hunting across the Arctic, the lore of Tristram starts to seem positively precious.

To hunt game out of need reveals human frailty in the face of an unforgiving land, an understanding that used to saturate menus that were the culinary equivalent of *vanitas* paintings. In *Two Bookes of Cookerie and Carving* (*c.* 1641), John Murrell set out a summer menu for 50. It called for a first course of twenty dishes including capons, pikes, partridges, wild ducks, quails, 'a Florentine of Puft-paste', a 'forced boyld meate', a hash of venison, a swan and a 'Fawne or Kid, with a pudding in his belly'. Evocative and literal, this last dish reminded jaded diners of the doe's gravid uterus and the nourishment held within, as well as the essential role of the cook who takes the raw flesh of wild animals and transforms it into a delicate, human thing: cuisine.

Kitagawa Utamaro, *Swallows and Pheasant*, 1790.

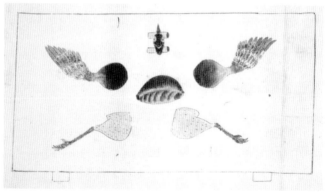

Shikin Miyazaki, *Ikuma School Technique for Carving a Pheasant*, 1799.

4
The Raw and the Cooked:
Making Your Own Meat

Who let that bloody brute in here?
George Orwell, 'A Hanging' (1931)

James Clavell's novel *Shōgun* (1975), set in seventeenth-century
feudal Japan, features a famous scene in which the Japanese
locals present their British guest, John Blackthorne, with a
pheasant. Pleased, Blackthorne orders the bird to be hung
for a few days so it can be properly aged according to British
custom. His decision has terrible consequences. Not only
are the locals disgusted by Blackthorne's plan to eat days-old
meat, but the gardener is so appalled that he takes the bird
down, knowing full well that he will be beheaded for his dis-
obedience. With dramatic literalism, the gardener's actions
demonstrate that palatability is less about taste buds than it is
about brain cells. In this case, however, the brain cells that
matter belong to Clavell, who used them to invent a Japanese
gardener so revolted by the thought of letting a carcass ripen
that he would rather die than allow the process to continue.

Is hung pheasant better than pheasant that is eaten right
away? Is aged beef merely rotten meat with a lofty price tag? It
is exquisitely futile to argue from the platform of taste, which

89

'An Animal Keeper Feeding Raw Meat to Lions in a Circus Cage as Spectators Watch', c. 1891.

is, nowadays, routinely folded into the cult of individualism. I like vanilla ice cream, you hate vanilla ice cream, and there you have it. But to find a hung pheasant disgusting does not reflect personal taste. Rather, it reflects the influence of several cultural taboos, one of which will be violated if the hung bird is eaten but not cooked. Broadly speaking, as noted by Claude Lévi-Strauss in his classic ethnographic study, *The Raw and the Cooked* (1964), it is impossible to understand categories such as 'raw', 'cooked', 'fresh' and 'decayed' without adopting the 'standpoint of a particular culture'. Many cultural myths stress that only animals eat raw meat. Thus wild lions eat warm gazelles, zoo tigers eat raw horsemeat, pet dogs eat kibble and progressive cats are going vegan, signalling their status as that of a petulant child permanently dependent on their parents. Correspondingly, it becomes a sign of humanness to eat highly 'cooked' foods, or foods that bear little to no resemblance to their original state as whole vegetable, whole fruit or whole animal. Thus the pinnacle of contemporary cuisine isn't a bowl of apples and barbecued ribs, but a foam made from morel mushrooms.

On the opposite end of the spectrum, some urban humans will only eat raw food, a practice called 'rawism', rejecting cultural artifice in order to practice a secular form of asceticism. Rawism seems diametrically opposed to the gastronomic impulse, yet it is merely a different expression of the same impulse: the atavistic fear of savagery. Children still delight in the nursery rhyme about

> Sing a song of sixpence
> A pocketful of rye
> Four and twenty blackbirds
> Baked in a pie.
> When the pie was opened

The birds began to sing
Wasn't that a dainty dish
To set before the king?

It describes a dish known through several historical descriptions, including Giovanni de Roselli's *Epulario, quale tratta del modo de cucinare ogni carne, ucelli, pesci* . . . (1549, translated into English in 1598 as *Epulario, or the Italian Banquet*). This cookbook contained a recipe 'to make pies so that birds may be alive in them and flie out when it is cut up'. This is the best and most refined of all foods: so raw that it refuses to be eaten, providing the guests with exceptional entertainment.

Only humans control fire, and thus cooking is a sacred act that distinguishes men from beasts. In myths, to steal fire from the gods is a task for heroes ranging from Prometheus of Greek mythology to Mátariśvan of the Rig Veda. As related in the *Shahnameh*, King Hushang spotted a monster 'with eyes like pools of blood and jaws whose smoke / Bedimmed the world'. He threw a stone at the monster, but missed. The stone made sparks when it struck a rock, and thus he discovered fire. The resulting celebration, called the Feast of Sada, was a popular subject for Persian artists, who typically showed an open fire surrounded by a variety of wild and domesticated birds and animals. Through fire, the poet Ferdowsi tells us, King Hushang 'civilized the world':

By Grace and kingly power domesticating
Ox, ass, and sheep he turned them to good use.
'Pair them', he said, 'use them for toil, enjoy
Their produce, and provide therewith your taxes'.

Dated two centuries earlier, another version of the Feast of Sada from *al-Āthār al-Bāqiya an al-Qurūn al-Khāliya* (The

Chronology of Ancient Nations, 1307) by al-Abu Rayhān al-Bīrunī shows a custom practised by rulers during Bahman, the tenth month. The catalogue entry for the illuminated manuscript indicates that rulers would 'celebrate by lighting fires and driving animals and birds into the flames while drinking and cavorting then ending the day by asking for God's vengeance on those who torment harmless creatures'.

These powerful and complex stories stress the transform-ative role of the wild animal roasting in the fire. One of the most important myths that Lévi-Strauss relates belongs to the Obaye tribe. The central actor in this Amazonian myth is a *preá* (*Cavia aperea*), the Brazilian guinea pig, which looks like a pet-shop guinea pig and is such an 'insignificant' creature, Lévi-Strauss tells us, that the natives don't consider it worth hunting. According to this myth, the jaguar's mother controls fire, and the animals try to steal it. One by one they fail, leaving only the *preá* to make the attempt. The little animal gets the jaguar to chase him, and convinces him that there is 'no healthier food than raw, bloody flesh'. The jaguar responds by tearing off the *preá*'s snout with his paw, leaving it with a squashed (human) face. Then the jaguar teaches the *preá* how to cook:

> Light a fire, put the meat on a stick, and grill it; if you have time, cook it in an oven that has been hollowed out in the ground and previously heated; put foliage around the meat to protect it, and earth and hot ashes on top.

The jaguar then teaches the *preá* how to make fire by rubbing together two sticks. It is a happy ending for the *preá* who, like humans, falls outside the food chain. He doesn't get eaten raw or cooked, and lives to tell the tale.

For adventurers, few challenges were more aggravating than losing the ability to make fire in very cold regions of the world.

The explorer David Hanbury repeatedly ran into this problem as he explored the 'barren' tundra near the Arctic Circle. As described in his memoir, *Sport and Travel in the Northland of Canada* (1904), he found himself confronted with temperatures that fell to −41°F/C at night, dwindling sightings of game animals (chiefly deer and rabbits) that they hunted as they travelled, and no wood because there were no trees to begin with. His team had run out of kerosene, and they had to collect moss to burn in hopes of boiling venison for supper. 'I have never yet got accustomed to eating meat raw', Hanbury confessed 'and I have to be very hungry to do it.' He found frozen meat too cold for the teeth and, oddly, too 'flabby' in taste, even while acknowledging that his meat was as hard as a rock.

But he wasn't describing its texture. He was describing its flavour. Hanbury and his team hunted game and ate on the move, so the practice of hanging the meat never came up as an option. Now, it is commonly said of game that it needs to be hung in order to tenderize and age the meat. It is also a requirement that is quibbled over and parsed in every venison cookbook and hunting blog. At the Oxford Food Symposium of 2004, the game-tasting lunch hosted by venison expert Nichola Fletcher played with these variables by including the following items:

Roe venison, not hung at all
Roe venison, hung fourteen days
Roe venison, bruised from bullet shot
Pheasant, marinated
Pheasant, not marinated
Pheasant, hung for ten to twelve days and marinated

Some hunters insist that a deer must be hung for at least two weeks. Others dismiss hanging as a waste of time, and recommend digging in immediately. Indeed, the *Ménagier de Paris* (1393) went so far as to argue with itself, offering advice regarding the merits of hanging a hare before preparing it for cooking.

Note that on a hare which is freshly taken and soon eaten the meat is more tender than a kept hare.

Item, a hare taken fifteen days previously is the best, as long as the sun has not touched it; that is to say, fifteen days in the depth of winter: in summer, six or eight days or more and without sun.

Item, know that if the hare is eaten when freshly taken, its meat is more tender, and there is no need to wash it, but roast it with its blood.

If a hare is taken two or three weeks before Easter, or at some other time when you want to save it, gut it and

John Feeney, *Winter Hare Taken in Maine*, 2012.

take out the entrails, then cut the skin on its head and break it, and make an opening in the head and remove the brain and fill the hole with salt and sew up the skin: it will keep for a month if hung by the ears.

The practice of salting the hare's brain and hanging it for a month in the warm spring, before the age of refrigeration, makes me wonder how anybody survived the Middle Ages. There are good scientific reasons for hanging the carcass, such as the explanation offered by Stanley and Adam Marianski in *Home Production of Quality Meats and Sausages* (2010). For large game such as deer, the tenderness drops about five hours after death, when rigor mortis sets in, and this will last until the sixth day, when rigor dissipates, and then it continues to tenderize until the fourteenth day. The meat must be kept at 34–38°F (1–3°C) for this process to be safe. This timetable may explain the conflicted advice offered by the *Ménagier de Paris*, which veers back and forth from 'freshly taken' to 'fifteen days' to 'freshly taken' again.

The dry facts of food science fail to convince many hunters who butcher their own game, whose local customs and family traditions tend to hold sway. On a certain level, the disagreements are really a tacit acknowledgement of the uniqueness of each animal, the importance of the hunter's skill and the intimate relationship between the quarry, the hunter and the land. Hearne describes a northern Native American practice of chasing a moose through deep snow until the animal is exhausted, at which point it can be killed with a knife. Because 'the animal must have been in a violent fever' after running for so many hours, the 'soft and clammy' flesh 'must have a very disagreeable taste, neither resembling fish, flesh, nor fowl', and he figures that it was 'ten times worse tasted than the spleen or milt of a bacon hog'. (In modern usage, 'milt' refers to the seminal fluid of fish and molluscs, which are delicacies in Russian, Japanese, and Sicilian cuisine.) Hearne concludes that the terrible taste was due to the moose's blood saturating its muscles. This phenomenon, plus great doses of testosterone, contributes to a gamey taste in males with large, impressive antlers. Some of this strong taste can be improved by hanging, but it is not guaranteed.

Recently, the disputed benefits of hanging came up in a sideways fashion with the half-serious question: 'What does sloth meat taste like?' If hanging a deer carcass for a week will improve the flavour as well as the texture, surely sloths, which spend their whole existence hanging off a branch, are meltingly delicious? In 2012 some American university students posed the question to The Explainer at Slate.com. The students reasoned that sloths hardly move at all, therefore their meat will be exceptionally tender. Alas, no. According to Brian 'The Explainer' Palmer, muscle tone does not directly impact the texture of the meat. He also cautions that is illegal to hunt sloths and only a few tribes indigenous to Brazil eat them, but Western researchers who have tried it anyway describe it as being 'slimy, chewy, and gamey'. In other words, it tastes like green venison taken off an old buck downed in full chase.

What all this suggests, then, is that young game animals, and small, young females in particular, are likely to be good eating if dressed and fully butchered within five hours of killing. These tasks are nearly impossible to accomplish if the carcass belongs to an old male, which is more work in general to render palatable to humans, irrespective of the species. The *Larousse Gastronomique* reports that, for example:

> [Bull] elephant meat is tough but tasty, provided that it is cooked for more than 15 hours or has been hung for a long

time in the open air. The feet, the heart and the trunk are of the greatest culinary interest; their flesh, which is muscular and gelatinous, resembles ox (beef) tongue.

An experienced chef will refuse a ten-point winter stag that has been chased all day with a pack of dogs, as the meat will be chewy and strong regardless of whether or not it has been hung. In the winter, deer rely on acorns, which affect the flavour of the fat. Thanks to the *Foxfire* series, an American oral history project that chronicles the folkways of Appalachia, we know that livestock pigs running loose in the forests of the southern USA rooted for acorns, which impart a rancid flavour to the bacon fat due to tannins. To solve this, Appalachian farmers would bring the pigs in, pen them and feed them a diet of grain and corn for two weeks before slaughter. It thus makes sense that the hunting schedules provided by the *Propre New Boke of Cookerye*, the *White House Cook Book* and other such cooking manuals were implicitly attentive to the local forage according to the four seasons. By contrast, the breeding period of a game animal, which is paramount today and regulated by law, hardly mattered at all.

The impact of age, sex and diet on the taste of wild meat seems to be important across the entire spectrum of game, from smallest of birds to the largest of large game. For Hearne, for example,

The flesh of the musk-ox nowa[da]ys resembles that of the Western buffalo, but is more like that or moose or elk; and the fat is of a clear white, slightly tinged with a light azure. The calves and young heifers are good eating, but the flesh of the bulls both tastes and smells so strongly of musk, as to render it very disagreeable.

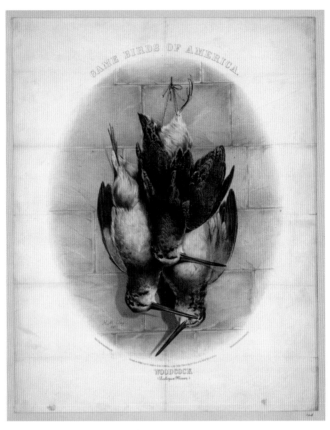

Hugh M. Clay, 'Woodcock (*Scolopax minor*)', from *Game Birds of America* (1861).

If a carcass wasn't properly aged, cooking techniques could act as a corrective. The chef could also work wonders on a bird that had perhaps been hanging too long, acquiring what Apicius called a 'goatish smell'. (He was firmly in the hanging camp, emphasizing that a hare must be hung a few days before it could be properly eaten.) One technique was to disguise the bad taste with even stronger flavours, such as immersing the meat in a concoction of pepper, lovage, thyme, dry mint, sage, dates, honey, vinegar, wine, broth, reduced must and mustard. The bird could simply be parboiled, Apicius counselled, or stuffed with crushed fresh olives, sewn shut, roasted, and the olives then removed and discarded. Tellingly, however, Apicius preferred to wrap his goaty birds in a bit of oiled dough and then roast them in the oven, which would preserve the fat, he said, resulting in a 'more luscious and nutritious' dish. These remarks imply that he didn't mind very ripe birds and quite possibly preferred them.

By contrast, Industrial Age cookbooks typically sought to reduce what Mrs Beeton called the 'haut goût', or the strong flavour of wildness. These quibbles over flavour are distinct from the texture of the meat which, regardless of how it is prepared, is always leaner and typically tougher than its domesticated equivalent. Discussions regarding this aspect of game meat are relatively recent, and speak to an emerging cultural norm that now expects 'good' meat to be hygienically prepared, thinly sliced and unresistingly tender. Today this expectation holds true even among the hardiest of adventure hunters: in an issue of the American magazine *Petersen's Hunting* (April–May 2012), hunter-cook Steve 'Meateater' Rinella points out that hunters like to 'brag about tough hunts, tough hikes, tough weather and tough shots', and they willingly endure extreme weather and choke down freeze-dried camp food as they pursue their quarry. Yet 'they cry like spoiled babies when they bite into a tough or gamey chunk of meat' they have carved off from their kill. In the mouth, wild meat suddenly refuses to cooperate, jolting the hunter into the unwelcome awareness that his secret sensibilities are girlishly tender.

The lesson here is that game animals don't automatically become game meat. Hung, the gutted game bird or animal is suspended in a liminal state between nature and culture, occupying an ambiguity that doesn't fully resolve itself until the meat becomes a meal. That meal is a test. The test is the taste. To pass the test, rig the game. In *Game Birds of India, Burma, and Ceylon* (1921), Edward Charles Stuart Baker rhapsodized at length about the joy of hunting game birds in a beautiful land (where no hunting laws applied to British colonials such as him). Chasing woodcock through the 'sombre pine forest, the sunlit copes', the hunter thrills when he finally hears the 'owl-like flip-flap of the brown bird's wings', and knows that he has found a brace to shoot. It is 'only when the cook has worked his will on the results of the day's bag' that the hunter remembers his accursed nature. 'Only man is vile', Baker quipped. His belly full of small, tender, young birds that don't need to be hung, he resumes hunting for more the next morning.

5

The Forlorn Table

In his *Compleat History of Animals and Minerals* (1661), Robert Lovell described the taste of 'Unicorne' meat as being terribly bitter. Pronouncing it unfit to be eaten, he went on to recommend consuming the horn as excellent medicine. 'It's much commended against pestilent fevers, and the bitings of mad Doggs, and other poysonous beastes, and also against wormes.' Lovell gives every impression of having actually eaten unicorn steaks as well as 'Indian Asse' which, he says, tastes just as bad. What he was actually consuming is open to speculation, but he probably wasn't trying to bamboozle his readers. (The same cannot be said of pranksters at the British Library, who on April Fool's Day in 2012 announced that a fourteenth-century cookbook by 'Geoffroy Fule' had been discovered, along with a recipe for cooking unicorn in cloves and garlic: 'Taketh one unicorne . . .'.) We may scoff at Lovell's gullible palate, but what if he ate the last unicorn on earth? The possibility is not as farfetched as it might seem. A list of the top ten new species of 2011, formulated by the International Institute for Species Exploration at Arizona State University, included a 'dead antelope' dubbed *Philantomba walteri*. The unique specimen of this new species was discovered in a West African bushmeat market. It was the first and last of its kind. Were its flesh tasted before being preserved for science, I should think that it, too, would have left a bitter taste behind.

Today, the dodo, the quagga and the Saudi gazelle also float like myths in the popular imagination. Long believed to have been a creature more fake than the unicorn, the dodo (*Raphus cucullatus*) was improbably confirmed to be a 'real' extinct animal after it was illustrated in *Alice's Adventures in Wonderland*. The front half of the quagga (*Equus quagga quagga*) was striped like a zebra, but its back half was plain. A taxidermied specimen of the quagga is now displayed near a model of the dodo in the Muséum National d'Histoire Naturelle, Paris, but its appearance is so alien to contemporary imaginations that it fills the speculative space vacated by the 'Fiji mermaid', the famous P. T. Barnum hoax which fused the tail of a fish to the torso of a juvenile monkey. The Saudi gazelle (*Gazella*

A quagga (*Equus quagga quagga*) at the London Zoo, 1870.

saudiya) has the ignominious distinction of being an animal that went extinct before it could be defined as a species. Adding insult to injury, it now lives on as a DNA sequence at the British Museum, which displays a different animal, the Dorcas gazelle (*G. dorcas*), as an example of what it mght have looked like.

These three modern creatures are now extinct, doomed by the unfortunate fact that they were delicious. They share the fate of Bechstein's macaw and some varieties of West Indian macaws, amazons and conures, all of which vanished through the 'persecution by the inhabitants for food'. This was ornithologist Walter Rothschild's assessment in *Extinct Birds* (1907), a dolorous work listing many birds that have disappeared from the face of the earth. Yet each disappearance is part of a complicated picture that implicates every human on the planet. Of the 10,000 species known to have become extinct in the twentieth century, the vast majority were snails, frogs, turtles and birds. We cannot blame French cuisine for this.

The recent case of the Przewalski wild horse (*Equus ferus przewalskii*) illustrates the complexities of the issues. Przewalski horses are extinct in the wild, with remaining specimens surviving only through breeding programmes in captivity. In 1998–9, a herd of 31 hybridized horses were reintroduced into the wild. One location was the 30-km Exclusion Zone around Chernobyl, where wildlife such as badgers, beavers, boars, lynx, wolves and a host of birds had surprised researchers by reappearing. The wild horse populations started to rebuild, nearly doubling in size until their numbers abruptly started to drop. In 2011, the BBC reported the suspicion that the horses were being poached, though whether by starving Ukrainians, black marketeers or rebounding wolves was impossible to say, because the area is a radioactive zone and will not be safe for human habitation for 20,000 years.

It's difficult to imagine a more artificial set of circumstances than a group of Mongolian wild horses plopped into a nuclear wasteland in the Ukraine, but the 38th Parallel separating the two Koreas presents the purest imposition of political will on the planet. Since the 1950s this 4-km-wide (2.5-mile) strip of land cutting across the peninsula has been essentially free from human contact, airspace included, turning it into a secular Garden of Eden from which man has been permanently exiled. As a result, it is rumoured that several possibly extinct species have been sighted there. (Ironically, one of the few places in Korea that allows hunting is Jeju Island, which has wildlife such as deer and boar as well as a private pheasant hunting preserve. It became known to foreigners as a hunting site thanks to the Korean War.) Either side of the 38th Parallel, armed soldiers line up like teeth. But inside the Korean Eden, Hodori the Tiger dances with the crane.

Both Chernobyl and the Korean Demilitarized Zone are wildernesses of a very peculiar kind, because their existence is profoundly unnatural. The forced evacuation of men from these violent sites is the paradoxical result of a deep belief in human dominion over nature, which remains stubbornly in place even when the failsafes fail and disorder escapes. In order to illustrate the fatal implications of that belief, science fiction writer H. G. Wells banished all 'brutes' from *A Modern Utopia* (1905). In this perfect, vegetarian world, there are no meats, no bugs and no pets. The botanist protests the ban by declaring that 'dogs are people too!' He fails to grasp that this was why Wells had to get rid of them.

To put the matter another way, one of the most famous cases of modern extinction through human agency is the dodo. Praised as 'the best game on the island' of Réunion by Sieur Dubois in 1674, the dodo was originally called

Dutch School, *Dodo*, 17th century, watercolour.

'walghvogel', meaning 'wallow bird' or 'loathsome bird', presumably in reference to its flavour. The revealing name was first used in the journal of Vice-admiral Wybrand van Warwijck, who visited the island with the Van Neck expedition in 1598:

> On their left hand was a little island which they named Heemskirk Island, and the bay it selve they called Warwick

Bay . . . finding in this place great quantity of foules twice as bigge as swans, which they call Walghstocks or Wallowbirdes being very good meat. But finding an abundance of pigeons & popinnayes [parrots], they disdained any more to eat those great foules calling them Wallowbirds, that is to say lothsome or fulsome birdes.

An account of Admiral Jacob van Neck's journey to the neighbouring island of Mauritius observes that the sailors used to call the dodo a walghvogel, 'for the reason that the longer and oftener they were cooked, the less soft and more insipid eating they became. Nevertheless their belly and breast were of a pleasant flavour and easily masticated.'

As with many game birds, the degree of palatability depends on the cut as well as the preparation. It's possible that dodos were excellent eating if the right person was doing the cooking. It's also possible that they tasted terrible, and their main appeal was that they were easy to catch. What cannot be debated is the fact that sailors ate dodos, as well as wild pigeons and parrots. Yet researchers have concluded that the dodo did not become extinct because it was hunted as game. The major culprits were hungry human companions, namely cats, rodents, pigs and dogs.

Wherever they go, pigs are enormously destructive of habitat. Rats and mice steal eggs, and cats are lethal to baby birds. The ability of household pets to obliterate wildlife was not lost on men practiced in the art of war. In *The Wonders of Nature and Art; or, a Concise Account of Whatever is Most Curious and Remarkable in the World* (1804), the Revd Thomas Smith described a devious tactic used by the eighteenth-century Spanish Armada to fight buccaneers. The Spanish had learned that pirates were hunting goats on the islands of Juan Fernández off the shores of Chile, and they relied on

Elmer Boyd Smith, *Robinson Crusoe Hunting Game Birds with Dog Tied to Post*, 1880–1943.

this meat to provision their ships. To hamper the pirates, the Spanish released packs of large dogs and let them loose on the islands. The tactic was successful: the number of dogs subsequently 'increased so fast', Smith commented, 'that they have destroyed all the goats in the accessible parts of the country'. The few goats that survived lived among 'crags and precipices' so high and dangerous that the dogs could not follow.

Yet the goats were also alien to the islands. Like the dogs, they were domesticated breeds that had gone feral. They had been introduced by the British sailor Alexander Selkirk, who was stranded there from 1705 to 1709, and is often credited with inspiring Daniel Defoe's novel *Robinson Crusoe* (1719). The Spanish dogs died out, but Selkirk's cats and rodents are still running loose, steadily bringing his island's few remaining endangered birds closer to extinction even as conservationists work madly to save them.

Floating in the South Pacific, this little bit of contested land might well be taken as a microcosm of the civilizing

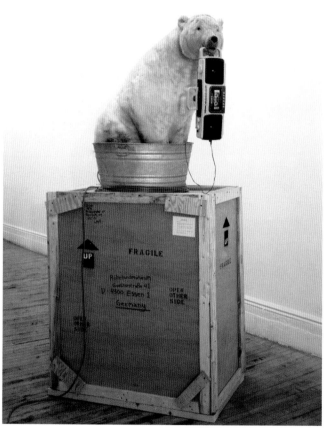

Mark Dion, *Polar Bear and Toucans*, 1991.

effect on the world. When civilization arrives, 'pure products go crazy', observed anthropologist James Clifford in *The Predicament of Culture* (1988). He was paraphrasing the famous first line of William Carlos Williams's poem 'To Elsie'(1923), in which Williams warned that romanticizing nature will not heal the psychic woes of modernity:

> . . . we eat filth
>
> while the imagination strains
> after deer
> going by fields of goldenrod in
>
> the stifling heat of September
> Somehow
> it seems to destroy us

Today, authentic 'wildness' is privileged to certain creatures, typically charismatic predators indigenous to human-hostile environments, such as such as jungle panthers and Arctic polar bears. Their association with remote geographies helps preserve the fiction of cultural purity, but the horror story is that humans leak everywhere.

Reality is messy. In everyday life, the lines between domesticated, wild, native, feral and foreign animals are remarkably blurred, and it is mostly cultural reflexes that determine how the status of an animal gets interpreted. A good example is the fallow deer, which has been hunted in Britain and Continental Europe for thousands of years. It's profoundly linked to British identity, yet it is not an indigenous species. Originally from Eurasia, fallow deer were introduced around the first century CE to Britain, where it has since proliferated. 'Ever since the Neolithic,' the Fallow Deer Project website explains, 'humans have selectively transported and maintained this elegant animal, taking it from its restricted native range in the eastern Mediterranean across Europe where it is now an established icon of stately homes.'

Now folded into a domestic idyll, the fallow deer has been fully absorbed into the British landscape where it roams as a naturalized element. This history cannot be willed away because the fallow deer came from somewhere else, for the meat itself helped construct and define social status among Normans. For example, medieval British recipe books repeatedly refer to the haunch of venison but not the shoulders because, anthropologist Naomi Sykes suggests, the shoulders were 'gifted' to the best hunter on the spot. It is an interesting thesis regarding the nature of alimentary prestige. Certainly there were exceptions, and it may be that this practice was specific to Britain. The medieval Polish recipe recovered by Maria Dembinska specifically invoked the shoulder of a stag (*jelerí*, which is to say, an adult male red deer), and not the 'much smaller' roe deer (*saran*). These nuances underscore the cultural specificity of 'venison' in terms of subspecies, sex, age, variety and preparation in the medieval imagination, much in the same way that 'filet mignon' and 'hamburger' encapsulate economic and culinary stratifications inside the fast-food nation.

Wenceslaus Hollar, *Coursing Fallow Deer*, later 17th century.

C. Petznick, *Game, Berlin, Germany*, 1895–1910.

Today, many advocates for heritage breeds of livestock argue that the best way to preserve vanishing lines is to promote their consumption as food, for sustainable practices must ensure the farmer's economic survival as well as the well-being of the animal. Though not exactly comparable, a full consideration of game meat must likewise address the complex interplay of local traditions and global economies that impacts wildlife. Globally speaking, for example, deer are not threatened, but there are numerous examples of modern extinctions of particular species within the deer family. Indigenous to China, Père David's deer is extinct in the wild, though some survive in captivity. In other instances, however, wild herds that were threatened due to human hunting are today thriving due to human intervention. The formerly overhunted American whitetails have rebounded so strongly that they are becoming nuisance animals again. In the U.S. alone, over 1.5 million deer annually become roadkill, giving rise to a new role for hunters as agents of responsible wildlife management.

In Australia, the role of 'deer' is played by kangaroos. 'One humorous gentleman whom I met in Melbourne', wrote hunter Birge Harrison in 1890, 'professed to regard the kangaroo as an entirely mythical animal deserving only to be classed with the sea serpent, the dragon, and the "bunyip" [a creature affirmed to live in swamps and billabongs]'. The meat had a 'delicate, gamey flavor', Harrison observed, 'something between that of venison and grouse'. The tail was a delicacy that could be roasted, boiled, braised, potted or stewed, but was especially delicious, Harrison said, when prepared as kangaroo-tail soup. But the precipitous drop in the nineteenth-century kangaroo population wasn't because too many cooks were out shooting their supper. It was the effect of government extermination programmes designed to rid the country of an animal that threatened the sheep industry. The government instituted programmes to restore the kan-

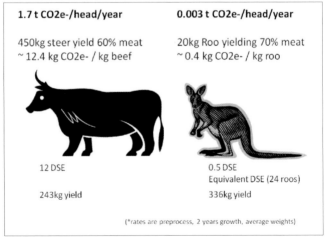

Cow vs Roo chart, giving details of meat yield and CO_2 usage.

Gad, 'Chef with Blunderbuss', from *Dictionnaire des pêcheurs et des chasseurs* (1965).

garoos after it became clear their numbers were too low. Ironically, Australia's kangaroo populations proceeded to rebound so strongly that they exceeded the ability of the land to sustain them, and they are now dying mass deaths due to starvation. Long a staple of the Aboriginal diet, kangaroo meat is now reappearing on restaurant menus, supplied by professional hunters culling wild herds with the blessing of wildlife biologists.

Elsewhere, highly endangered large game animals as the scimitar-horned oryx are now thriving on hunting ranches such as those found in Texas, which has effectively been turned into an enormous game preserve, with over 125 different exotic species from Asia, Africa and Europe. Some of these animals have thus been brought back from the brink of extinction in their native lands, and the ranchers affirm that they are performing conservation. Only that justification is new. The power dynamic is very old. Historically, rulers routinely annexed exotic and native game animals to their households on a very large scale. According to Suetonius, the Roman emperor Nero built an estate called the Golden House, which included 'a garden consisting of plowed fields, vineyards, pastures, and woodlands, in which every variety of domestic and wild animal roamed'. In Old Kingdom Egypt (2686–2181 BCE), semi-domesticated animals included the oryx, gazelle, hartebeest and addax, many of which were depicted being hand-fed and wearing collars around their necks at the mastaba of Mereruka in Saqqara. One bas-relief shows a plump hyena (*Hyaena hyaena*) on its back, trussed, being fed by hand. It has been argued that this hyena is, rather, an aardwolf (*Proteles cristata)*, which is a small member of the Hyaenidae family.

Aardwolves are relatively obscure, whereas hyenas are universally loathed. In *Contemporary Land Mammals of Egypt* (1980), Dale Osborn and Ibrahim Helmy report that striped hyenas are eaten by Egyptian peasants, certain Arabian Bedouins, Palestinian labourers, Sinai Bedouins and Tuaregs. Their flesh is sold at market, they note, and the primary buyers were religious leaders. They emphasize that when hyenas are eaten, it is typically not as food but as magical medicine. (The body parts of certain wild animals, such as deer penis and rhinoceros horn, have long been invested with quasi-magical properties and can fetch enormous prices on the black market. The topic of criminal poaching is outside the purview of this book, but it must be mentioned insofar as it is an acute global problem.) I am nonetheless told by cookbook editor Simon O'Rourke, of Rabat, Morocco, that hyena and aardwolf meat is 'everywhere', and it tastes a lot like goat.

The tradition of semi-domesticating wild animals goes back for millennia. But this is a blip compared to the length of the human relationship with reindeer, a relationship that cannot be disentangled from the history of humanity itself. Simultaneously intimate and obscure, that ongoing relationship illuminates the complex cultural constraints imposed on animals that become 'food'. In 1991, the menu for Pectopah

Šašlik (Šašlik Restaurant), a stylish Russian restaurant in Helsinki, Finland, featured signature dishes such as 'Genuine Russian roast bear', 'Wild Boar roasted à la Kiev' and 'Juicy reindeer fillet Vostok'. These delicacies did not come cheap: at 420 markka, the 'bear fillet rarity' was three times more expensive than an order of 'genuine black caviar', and four times more expensive than the main course of reindeer meat. 'Bear and wild boar dishes [are] not always available', the menu noted, but no such caveat was attached to reindeer fillets or chicken dishes on the menu.

This was due to the fact that reindeer is not game in the traditional sense in Finland, because it is not procured from hunted wild animals. In Finland, reindeer are semi-domesticated, a relationship that remains in parts of Russia as well as Scandinavia in general. Outside of these regions, however, reindeer is not commonly thought of as a livestock animal that makes regular appearances at the dinner table. In winter 2011, a public relations flap in London inadvertently shone a spotlight on the geography of cultural taboo. The upscale British retailer Harvey Nichols made international news when it offered reindeer pâté as a seasonal gourmet treat, prompting the animal rights group Vegetarian International Voices for Animals (VIVA) to mount a vigorous protest. Instead, VIVA's attack served as free advertising, and the reindeer pâté flew off the shelves. Harvey Nichols professed to be mystified by the fuss, because the very fact that the tins were being offered for legal commercial sale meant that the meat could not be wild. It was farmed in Sweden.

Understood as a food commodity, reindeer pâté is no different from tinned beef. But meat is only straightforward to the starving. For just about everyone else, meat is a vexed substance precisely because it used to be an animal. What kind of animal the meat used to be makes all the difference,

Céline Clanet, 'Sámi Herder and Reindeer', from *Máze* series, *c.* 2005.

because every creature on this earth occupies a particular place inside a cultural order. Though bossy, cultural orders are not universal. Thus horsemeat is despised by some cultures yet embraced by others, and the cow, held sacred in India, is consumed around the world on the hoof as just another fast food. In developed-world settings, the practice of farming wild animals has surged in response to rising interest in traditional game meats such as venison. Largely a result of the 'locavore' (local food), 'slow food' and 'back-to-earth' movements that have been gaining steady traction since the 1970s, the newest permutations cast game meat as an ethical food that also possesses superior health benefits.

Such meat evacuates wildness in the name of preservation, denaturing the very thing it is trying to save. It is a devil's bargain, but one that, increasingly, it seems necessary to make.

Much like bats (a 'bird with fur'), salamanders (a 'snake with legs') and other 'supernatural' creatures damned for their deviant ways, the semi-domesticated animal challenges the contemporary brain. We don't know whether to eat a reindeer, or to pet it. Today, reindeer are farmed in Scandinavia, and semi-domesticated by indigenous peoples of the Arctic Circle such as the Sámi and Chukchi, who have developed extraordinary relationships with them. Because they are traditional reindeer herders, they are semi-nomadic, and migrate along with the reindeer. Largely located in the northernmost reaches of Norway and Finland, the Sámi culture is under stress due to increasing temperatures in the region that are directing affecting the people and their herds. The reindeer in artist Céline Clanet's photographs are not wild in the traditional sense, she emphasizes, because they are accompanied by a herder. Though the reindeer run free on the tundra, they are only 'game' insofar as they are not penned.

The Chukchi live on the Chukchi Peninsula, part of Russia. Like the Sámi, they are nomadic herders whose relationship to reindeer dates back to prehistory. In 2012, Petr Kaurgin of the Turvaurgin tribe in northeastern Siberia had been asked to speak at the Intergovernmental Panel on Climate Change being held in Australia. According to Stephen Leahy, writing for *National Geographic* magazine, 'Kaurgin and his family manage a herd of 50,000 reindeer, but they can no longer migrate to the rich grasses on the Arctic coast in summer because the ground is now too soft.' This is the effect of the melting permafrost, which they have been directly experiencing for the past twenty years. Their way of life is imminently doomed, yet the Sámi and the Chukchi have been herding, hunting and eating reindeer venison for tens of thousands of years. 'After all, the Chukchi have words for mammoth', said Tero Mustonen, the head of the village in Selkie, Finland. 'They have oral knowledge of how to hunt and cook mammoths.'

It is because the Sámi and Chukchi have always lived with the reindeer that outside observers have such a difficult time giving a coherent name to this relationship. It is not an asymmetrical power balance but a coeval one. Fully interdependent, this relationship doesn't correspond to modern farming, which turns animals into cultivated produce, and it doesn't correspond to the conventional terms of hunting, which imposes a hierarchy where animals are always the quarry. When the reindeer suffer, these humans suffer too. The animals are not pets. These nomadic herders eat the reindeer and wear their fur. Reindeer and humans live on the land. It is cold. From a distance, it is beautiful.

Whether geographic, cultural or historical, distance makes it easy to aestheticize their existence, for which reason it is important not to smother the nomadic herder's life with a self-serving sauce of spiritual essentialism. Hunting cultures of all kinds are susceptible to this kind of mythification. Consider a Native American Yokut tale about hunting for venison:

> The eagle called Hoey, the Deer, and told him, 'Hoey, you are going to be good meat for the new people [humans], they are going to kill you but, as soon as they do, you will leave your meat for them and go away and live again. You will not die.'

But of course, Hoey dies. He's as dead as a dormouse, a game animal that used to be coveted as a culinary delicacy. It is because of the mythicizing engine that the claim '"Vegetarian" is a Native American word for "bad hunter"' can be much repeated and readily accepted as authentic tribal wisdom. As best I can tell, it started as a joke invented by the American television writer Andy Rooney. The flip side of the coin is the tourist's position of moral superiority over hunters marin-ated in ignorance. Working as a Peace Corp volunteer on the Ivory Coast in 2006, reporter Petra Cahill had a piece of 'the most succulent, salty piece of meat' that she had ever tasted. 'I immediately asked, "what is that?" The response was "Hippopotame". I said, "What?!"' The criminal poaching of large game is rampant in Africa, she noted. Yet, to her perplexity, the fact that their populations were being deci-mated by trophy profiteers somehow didn't stop the locals from eating them. Or stop her, for that matter. She just didn't participate in the salvage, help move the carcass or prepare the meat. But she did eat it, marvelling at her own gastron-omic bravery.

John Feeney, *Moose Hunt, Bethel, Maine*, 2010.

J.C.W., 'A Game Crop is a Community Asset', 1936/7, poster.

To save the species, eat it. It is not as contradictory a claim as it seems, though it is not without consequences for cooks and other creatures. That species of frogs and snails are becoming extinct at an astonishing rate bothers few who shop for groceries, because it has no impact on middle-class plates. Out of mouth, out of mind. If modern men 'were told that they must kill before they may cook', Vehling had wryly noted in 1936, 'that might spoil the appetite and dinner joy of many a tender-hearted devourer of fellow-creatures'. Thus Henry David Thoreau chomped his way through the Maine woods, complaining every step of the way about those horrible Indians

Yoshitoshi Taiso, *Moon over Jogan Hall of the Palace*, c. 1880.

who were hunting animals to feed him. He also noted that moose meat, 'which is more like beef than venison, is common in Bangor [a town in northern Maine] market', which he visited in 1853. In the United States, wild venison is now illegal to sell, and the hunting of moose is limited by a stringent lottery system. The Maine moose in the photograph on p. 121 is a young bull with spikehorns. The rack is unsuitable for mounting as a trophy. Visually, it's an unimpressive specimen. But in the eyes of a cook, this bull is ideal, neither gamey nor tough. Its venison also bears little resemblance to beef, which is probably an indication that beef has become softer, fattier and blander in the intervening 160 years since Thoreau ate moosemeat, due to market forces pushing standardization.

Recently, a rash of hunter-cooks has emerged, publishing memoirs and starring in reality television shows about hunting for food. Some are acolytes of Michael Pollan, who concluded *The Omnivore's Dilemma* (2006) by going on a guided feral pig hunt. But Pollan is a writer, not a hunter. The canned culinary hunt more or less starts with the kill, which drives the storyline that readers and viewers expect. In everyday practice, however, a hunt is an exercise in failure. Again and again the quarry will refuse to show itself, and the hunter will return home empty-handed and hungry, forced to eat leftover beans while she studies the land, sights in her gun and revises the approach. This makes a terrible story, so the general public never hears about it. I have yet to meet a generational hunter who is not acutely aware that relying on game animals as a primary source of food cannot be sustained, because hunting does not come with guarantees, and one human eats a lot. This is why hunter-gatherer societies are nomadic: nature is a cornucopia only in poetry.

In hunting (which is not poaching), the individual dies, but the species lives. But when a species disappears, countries starve.

In 1958, Mao Zedong's 'Great Sparrow Campaign' mobilized the entire country of China into exterminating the Eurasian tree sparrow, which was, like the passenger pigeon in the u.s., demonized as an agricultural pest. Men, women and children happily netted, shot and trapped the birds, stealing their eggs to disrupt their nesting patterns, and banging loudly on tins until the birds died from noise exhaustion. The passenger pigeon went extinct. The Eurasian tree sparrow almost did. In China, the consequences were doubly tragic, because although the sparrows ate grain, they also ate insects. In the absence of sparrows, the locusts swarmed. The decimation of crops through insect activity became a significant factor contributing to the Great Chinese Famine (1958–61). In three years, approximately 30 million people died of starvation.

Call it the Sparrows' Revenge. The death of wildlife dooms humans, who would really rather not think about it, preferring instead to turn it all into a silly lark. Lewis Carroll had spelled it out literally:

> In the midst of the word he was trying to say,
> In the midst of his laughter and glee,
> He had softly and suddenly vanished away –
> For the Snark *was* a Boojum, you see.

It is our fault if we dismiss these words as childish whimsy. Of the modern extinction of the passenger pigeon, the *Encyclo - pedia Smithsonian* stated the political reality bluntly: 'The interests of civilization, with its forest clearing and farming, were diametrically opposed to the interests of the birds.' It concluded that the passenger pigeons would have become extinct anyway due to loss of habitat; the 'wanton slaughter of the birds only sped up the process'. The culprit is not human hunt - ing, but the phrase that catches the imagination is 'wanton slaughter', not the vague, elusive 'interests of civilization', marching inexorably forward since the Age of Exploration. And so blame continues to be assigned to hunters, when the actual culprit is hubris.

Over three centuries ago, in 1671, the fabulist Antoine Furetière had warned about what happens when the civilizing process goes unchecked. A king is on a difficult stag hunt. Once he has the stag at bay, the king vows to make the 'rebellious subject' suffer. He takes his anger out on the forest, sending 2,000 woodsmen to cut down the trees which had got in his way. Sometime later, the king decides to hunt again. Instead of a forest, he finds only a lovely field, incapable of supporting wildlife.

> What happened? The knight
> Wanting to hunt once again
> There found a truly pretty sight
> But didn't find any game.

Recipes

Stuffed Dormouse

—from *De re coquinaria*, Book VIII: *Quadrupeds*, late fourth to early fifth century

Dormouse: it is stuffed with a mash of pork and dormouse trimmings, pounded together with pepper, nuts, and silphium [also known as laser, an extinct plant believed to have been similar in taste to asafoetida]. Boil the stuffed dormouse in the stock pot, or put it in an earthen pot and roast it in the oven.

Rechhawbt (Head of Roe Deer)

—from *The Ambras Recipe-collection of Cod. Vind. 5486*, in *Food in the Middle Ages: A Book of Essays* (New York and London, 1995)

If you wish to make a good dish from a roe's head, simmer it until the meat falls off the bones. Chop the meat finely, and mix it with other chopped meat. Then take the skull bones, arrange the deer brain between them and cover them with an omelet. Cover the other bones with finely chopped meat. Then spice the dish and roast it, being careful to not to add too much salt. Serve the roe's head with a *ziseidel*, or with a light pepper sauce, etc.

Widgeon, Known as the Sparrow Hawk
—from *An Anonymous Andalusian Cookbook of the 13th Century*, trans.
Charles Perry

Cut the widgeon through all its joints into two pieces and put it in a pot; take gizzards of chicken and widgeon and clean them and cut them as fine as you can; throw in the pot with a spoon of *murri*, a head of garlic and two spoons of fresh oil, a stalk of rue, another of thyme, pepper, caraway, coriander both green and dried, a little onion and the whites of four eggs; beat well and throw a spoon of it in the pot and with the rest make meatballs and reserve some of it for the covering; cook the meatballs in the pot and stir the pot on all sides until the grease is properly cooked. Then take the whites of four eggs and beat with the rest of the filling, a bit of sifted flour and some pepper and cover the contents of the pot with it. You will have cooked the yolks of the eggs before this. Then arrange it on the platter, decorate with the meatballs and the yolks, and serve it, God willing.

To Bake Veneson
—from *A Propre New Booke of Cokery* (England, 1545)

Take nothing but pepper and salte but let it have inough and if the Veneson be lene lard it through with bakon.

Red Deer to Make: Or Make Beef Look Like It
—from *The Whole Duty of a Woman; or, a Guide to the Female Sex*
(England, 1696)

Parboyl it, and Press it, and let it ly all night in Red Wine, and a small quantity of Vinegar, then lard it thick, and season it with Pepper, Salt, Cloves, Mace and Nutmeg, or if you will, a little Ginger finely beaten, then lay it into your Pye or Pasty, with store of Butter; let it be well soak'd, and when you draw it out of the Oven, pour in at the Vent, Butter, Nutmeg, Sugar and a little

Ginger, beaten together; and so put it into the Oven again half an hour, and thus you may make Tender Beef pass for Venison.

How to Cook an Elephant

—from Samuel White Baker, *The Nile Tributaries of Abyssinia, and the Sword Hunters of the Hamran Arabs* (London, 1867)

Although the flesh of the elephant is extremely coarse, the foot and trunk are excellent, if properly cooked. A hole should be dug in the earth, about four feet deep, and two feet six inches in diameter, the sides of which should be perpendicular; in this a large fire should be lighted, and kept burning for four or five hours with a continual supply of wood, so that the walls become red-hot. At the expiration of the blaze, the foot should be laid upon the glowing embers, and the hole covered closely with thick pieces of green wood laid parallel together to form a ceiling; this should be covered with wet grass, and the whole plastered with mud, and stamped tightly down to retain the heat. Upon the mud, a quantity of earth should be heaped, and the oven should not be opened for thirty hours, or more. At the expiration of that time, the foot will be perfectly baked, and the sole will separate like a shoe, and expose a delicate substance that, with a little oil and vinegar, together with an allowance of pepper and salt, is a delicious dish that will feed about fifty men.

Beeatee

—from Samuel Hearne, *A Journey from Prince of Wales's Fort in Hudson's Bay to the Northern Ocean in the Years 1769, 1770, 1771 & 1772* (London, 1795)

Of all the dishes cooked by those people [Native Canadians], a *beeatee* as it is called in their language, is certainly the most delicious, at least for a change, that can be prepared from a deer only, without any other kind of ingredient. It is a kind of haggis, made with the blood, a good quantity of fat shred small, some of the tenderest of the flesh, together with the heart and lungs cut, or more commonly torn into small shivers; all of which is put into the stomach, and roasted, by being suspended before the fire by a string. Care must be taken that it does not get too much heat at first, as the bag would thereby be liable to be burnt, and the contents be let out. When it is sufficient done, it will emit steam, in the same manner of a fowl or a joint of meat; which is as much to say, Come, eat me now: and if it be taken in time, before the blood and other contents are too much done, it is certainly a most delicious morsel, even without pepper, salt, or any other seasoning.

Salmi of Game

—from Mrs F. L. Gillette and Hugo Ziemann, *White House Cook Book* (Chicago, 1887)

This is a nice mode of serving the remains of roasted game, but when a superlative salmi is desired, the birds must be scarcely more than half roasted for it. In either case, carve them very neatly, and strip every particle of skin and fat from the legs, wings and breasts; bruise the bodies well, and put them with the skin and other trimmings into a very clean stewpan. If for a simple and inexpensive dinner, merely add to them two sliced onions, a bay-leaf, a small blade of mace and a few peppercorns; then pour in a pint or more of good veal gravy, or strong broth, and boil it briskly until reduced nearly half; strain the gravy, pressing the bones well to obtain all the flavor; skim off the fat, add a little cayenne and lemon juice, heat the game very gradually in it, but do not on any account allow it to boil; place pieces of fried bread around a dish, arrange the birds in good form in the centre, give the sauce a boil, and pour it on them.

Passenger Pigeon Pot Pie

—from Margaret H. Mitchell, *The Passenger Pigeon in Ontario* (Toronto, 1935)

To make pot pie of them, line the bake-kettle with a good pie crust; lay out your birds, with a little butter on the breast of each, and a little pepper shaken over them, and pour in a tea cupful of water – do not fill your pan to full; lay in crust, about half an inch thick, cover your lid with hot embers and put a few below. Keep your bake-kettle turned carefully, adding more hot coals on the top, till the crust is cooked. This makes a very savoury dish for a family.

Kangaroo Tail Soup

—from 'the late 1800s, from our Grandmother's recipe book'. Recipe courtesy of Irene Brewer, curator of recipes at www.oldaussierecipes.com, who says, 'Kangaroo meat is very rich and high in protein . . . Properly cooked, the dish is most delicious.'

2 kangaroo tails

butter

2 carrots

4 diced onions

handful mixed herbs

450 g (1 lb) diced stewing steak

salt and pepper

2.85 l (6 pints) water

Chop tails at joints and brown in butter. Add carrots and onions and brown. Into a large pot place tail joints, vegetables, herbs, diced steak and add salt and pepper to taste. Add water, bring to boil then simmer for 3–4 hours. Remove tail joints and strain stock through sieve (forcing through with a spoon). Thicken soup with flour, return kangaroo tail joints and simmer for another 10–15 minutes. Serve with buttered bread, toast or damper. Note – kangaroo meat is quite lean.

Wild Rabbit Roast

—from Paula Lee, *Deer Hunting in Paris: A Memoir of God, Guns, and Game Meat* (San Francisco, 2013)

2 wild rabbits, skinned and jointed, tenderloins set aside
450 g (1 lb) bacon
2 yellow onions, thinly sliced
1 tablespoon celery powder
1 bottle dry white wine
1 tablespoon vegetable oil
salt and pepper to taste
butter
curly leaf parsley

Clean and joint the rabbits. Lay out the pieces in a large shallow baking dish and marinate in half the bottle of white wine for three hours at room temperature. (On a fresh rabbit, this step can be skipped. Do not use red wine.) Cut the bacon strips into thirds, and sauté at medium temperature until the fat is released but the strips are still soft. Remove the bacon from the pan and place in a bowl; set aside. Discard the marinade. Remove the tenderloins and set aside. Brown the rabbit joints in the bacon fat, then lay the pieces out flat in a lightly oiled baking dish. Do not discard the fat.

Add vegetable oil to the pan and sauté the onions until soft and translucent. Add the celery powder and remove from the heat. Drape the cooked bacon over the rabbit joints, covering all exposed surfaces. Top with onions, and then pour in the rest of the wine. Roast at 175°C (350°F) for an hour and a half, or until the wine has cooked off and bacon is crispy. Quickly sauté the tenderloins in butter and add to the rest of the meat. Remove from pan and serve, finishing with freshly cracked pepper and sprigs of curly parsley.

Serves 2–4

Cajun Grilled Alligator Kabobs

—from Skipper's Smokehouse, Tampa, Florida. Recipe courtesy of
Skipper's catering manager, Vicky Dodds.

450 g (1 lb) alligator meat
1 medium onion
cherry tomatoes
1 green pepper
8 whole mushrooms
(or any of your own favourite vegetables)
1 can (355 ml) orange juice
110 ml (1½ cup) readymade teriyaki sauce
cajun seasoning, or seasoned salt plus cayenne pepper

Cut alligator (available at Skipper's Smokehouse in Tampa; 813-
977-6474) into 1-inch cubes and marinate in orange juice and
teriyaki 6 to 24 hours. Use 8 wooden skewers (soak them in water
for at least a half hour before putting meat and veggies on them
to help prevent the wood from catching on fire) and skewer meat
alternately with chunks of onion, pepper, tomatoes and mushrooms, or your choice of veggies. Place kabobs on hot grill and
baste with marinade. Cook 2 to 3 minutes total, turning once.
Sprinkle with cajun seasoning to taste.
Serves 8 appetizer-size portions or 4 dinner portions

Venison with Cranberry-Port Relish

—from Anne Bramley, *Eat Feed Autumn Winter* (New York, 2008),
p. 97. Recipe courtesy of Anne Bramley, www.eatfeed.com. Anne says
these are her favourite flavours.

240 ml (1 cup) ruby port
¼ cup (35 g) dried currants
4 juniper berries
2 teaspoons minced fresh thyme
1 teaspoon freshly ground black pepper
1 teaspoon salt

2 tablespoons olive oil
2 racks venison, 4 ribs per rack, trimmed between bones
(450–700g / 1 to 1½ lb each)
120 ml (½ cup) beef broth
1 cup fresh cranberries
2 tablespoons packed light brown sugar

Preheat the oven to 220°C / 425°F. In a small saucepan, gently heat the port. Do not let it reach a simmer. Remove from the heat and add the currants. Set aside to soak.

Mix together the juniper berries, thyme, pepper, salt and olive oil. Let steep for 10 minutes to meld the flavours. Brush evenly over the venison. Arrange racks in a roasting pan facing each other so that the bones interlock and each rack has as much surface area exposed as possible. Roast until the internal temperature is 50°C / 125°F for rare, 20 to 30 minutes, depending on the size of the racks. Remove from the oven and transfer the racks to a serving platter to rest for 15 minutes. Tent with foil.

Drain the currants, reserving the port. Set the roasting pan across 2 burners on the stovetop. Turn each burner to medium-high. Add the port and beef broth to deglaze the pan. Scrape up any brown bits as you stir. Bring to a boil. Cook until the liquid is reduced to 180 ml / ¾ cup, about 10 minutes. Reduce the heat to medium-low and add the cranberries and brown sugar. Cook, stirring occasionally, until the cranberries are soft and you have a relish consistency, about 7 minutes. Add the currants.

Carve the venison into chops by slicing between the ribs. Serve with the relish.

Serves 4

A Canadian One-dish Meal

—Nathan Kowalski, author of *Hunting and Philosophy*.
Recipe courtesy of Helen Kowalski. Nathan Kowalski calls this
'the ultimate bachelor staple'.

In a casserole dish, layer 5 sliced potatoes, 1 chopped onion, 4 sliced
carrots and some salt (I used seasoning salt, use whatever spices you
want!). Top with a coiled deer sausage, thawed fully if previously
frozen. Mix 1 can of tomato soup with 1 can of water and pour it
over the top. Add plenty of pepper and bake for 1.5 hours at 175°C
(350°F).
Serves 1 bachelor

Grouse with Apples

—courtesy of Rex Croateau, Bryant Pond, Maine

Sauté Macintosh or Cortland apples over medium heat in a large
skillet with a generous knob of butter, until apples are soft but
not mushy. Remove from pan, add a little more butter, raise to high
heat and sear the breasts of a grouse. Lower heat to medium and
sauté until just cooked through. Do not overcook. Sprinkle with
chopped green (spring) onions, and serve with warm applesauce.

Fire Pit Roasted Aardwolf

—courtesy of Simon O'Rourke, Rabat, Morocco

Bury the beast in a smouldering pit of hot coals for about 18
hours with lots of onions and garlic on top. Also works on hyena
and wildebeest.

Impala Sosaties (Kebabs)

A traditional South African recipe from FunkyMunky.co.za. Recipe courtesy of Peter Thomas.

2 kg (4.5 lb) leg of impala, boned
32 dried apricots, soaked
2 onions, blanched and cut into chunks

Marinade
1 tablespoon mustard powder
125 ml (½ cup) tomato ketchup
1 tablespoon soy sauce
2 tablespoons peach chutney
6 cloves garlic, chopped
salt and milled black pepper

For the marinade, mix ingredients until smooth.

Carefully cube the impala flesh. Thread onto kebab skewers or sticks, alternately with apricots (4 to a skewer) and onion chunks. Marinate the sosaties for at least one day.

Charcoal grill for approximately 6 minutes, turning constantly. *Serves 2–4*

Select Bibliography

Allsen, Thomas T., *The Royal Hunt in Eurasian History*
(Philadelphia, PA, 2006)
Animal Studies Group, *Killing Animals* (Urbana, IL, 2006)
Beaver, Daniel, *Hunting and the Politics of Violence before the English
Civil War* (Cambridge, 2008)
Berry, Edward, *Shakespeare and the Hunt: A Cultural and Social
Study* (Cambridge, 2001)
Carnell, Simon, *Hare* (London, 2010)
Clutton-Brock, Juliet, *The Walking Larder: Patterns of
Domestication, Pastoralism, and Predation* (London, 1989)
Cosey, Herbert C., and Dwight Eisnach, *What the Slaves Ate:
Recollections of African American Foods and Foodways from the
Slave Narratives* (Santa Barbara, CA, 1999)
Dembinska, Maria, *Food and Drink in Medieval Poland*
(Philadelphia, PA, 1999)
Dumas, Alexandre, *Le Grand dictionnaire de cuisine* (Paris, 1872)
Fletcher, John, *Deer* (London, 2013)
Freedman, Paul, ed., *Food: A History of Taste* (Berkeley and
Los Angeles, CA, 2007)
Fudge, Erica, *Brutal Reasoning: Animals, Rationality, and Humanity
in Early Modern England* (Ithaca, NY, 2006)
Hache-Bisette, François, and Denis Saillard, eds, *Gastronomie et
identité culturelle française* (Paris, 2007)
Kennedy, Diana, *Oaxaca al Gusto: An Infinite Gastronomy*
(Austin, TX, 2010)

Ortega y Gasset, José, *Meditations on Hunting* [1942]

Rinella, Steven, *American Buffalo: In Search of a Lost Icon*
(New York, 2008)

Spang, Rebecca, *The Invention of the Restaurant: Paris and Modern
Gastronomic Culture* (Cambridge, MA, 2001)

Tuan, Yi-Fu, *Dominance and Affection: The Making of Pets*
(New Haven, CT, 2004)

Walker, Brett, *The Lost Wolves of Japan* (Seattle, WA, 2000)

Warnes, Andrew, *Savage Barbecue: Race, Culture, and the Invention
of America's First Food* (Atlanta, GA, 2008)

Websites and Associations

Environment and Ecology

A resource site with links to research studies on the practice and impact of hunting, run by the Norwegian Institute for Nature Research (NINA), in Norwegian and English
www.nina.no

On the archaeology of fallow deer in the UK and Europe, see the Fallow Deer Project/Dama International, based at the University of Nottingham, UK
www.fallow-deer-project.net

To learn more about reindeer in Siberia (in English, with links to Russian language sites)
www.eYakutia.com

Eating

A resource site regarding the crisis of subsistence hunting in Africa, with links, run by the World Wildlife Fund
www.worldwildlife.org

An online game meat course offered by British chef Hugh
Fearnley-Whittingstall
www.rivercottage.net

'A Mindful Carnivore', a blog written by an American
vegetarian-turned-hunter
www.tovarcerulli.com

'Hunter Angler Gardener Cook', a blog written by Hank Shaw,
a hunter-chef
www.honest-food.net

Hunting Clubs and Associations

Boone and Crockett Club, USA
www.boone-crockett.org

Confederation of Hunters Associations, South Africa
www.chasa.co.za

European Bowhunting Federation
www.europeanbowhunting.org

International Hunter Education Association
www.ihea-usa.org

Acknowledgements

Many people contributed to the writing of this book. For input and support along the way, I thank Bill Lawrence, Simon O'Rourke, Caroline Rothwell, Anne Bramley, Nathan Kowalski, Rex Croateau, Matt Carrano, Vicky Dodds, Peter Thomas, Irene Brewer, Jane Pollard, Dorthea Sartain, Olga Robak, Jennifer Davis, Anja Bryszki, Naomi Sykes, Sarah Biggs, Bertrand Laurence and Victoria Reynolds. For the privilege of reproducing visual material from their oeuvre, I am indebted to John Feeney, Amy Stein, Mark Dion and Céline Clanet. This book would not exist without the support of series editor Andrew Smith, as well as the staff at Reaktion Books. For their cheerful willingness to endure my cooking experiments, I owe a special thanks to my family.

Photo Acknowledgements

The author and the publishers wish to express their thanks to the below sources of illustrative material and/or permission to reproduce it.

From Jehoshaphat Aspin, *A Familiar Treatise on Astronomy* (1825): p. 25; from *Brehm's Life of Animals* (1927): p. 28; Bridgeman Art Library: p. 50; after Pieter Brueghel the Elder, *Luxuria* (1558): p. 49; after Theodore de Bry: p. 82; Celine Clanet: p. 118; Photo courtesy of Ctac [you are free: to share, copy, distribute and transmit this image under the following conditions: (1) you must attribute it to 'Ctac' but may not suggest that 'Ctac' endorses you or your use of the image; (2) if you alter, transform, or build upon this image, you may distribute the resulting work under the above conditions]: p. 33; from *Der ander Theil/ der Newlich erfundenen Landtschafft Americæ* (1575): p. 77; from *Dictionnaire des pechuers et des chasseurs* (1965): p. 115; John Feeney: pp. 96, 121; from Hugh M. Clay, *Game Birds of America* (1861): p. 100; Library of Congress: pp. 10, 11, 14, 19, 29, 39, 40, 41, 44, 45, 58, 59, 61, 64, 65, 70, 81, 88, 90, 91, 107, 109, 122, 123; from Martinet, *The Cook* (1780): p. 76; from Konrad von Megenberg, *Buch der Natur* (1481): p. 9; Shutterstock: p. 6; courtesy of Amy Stein: p. 17; from Alexander Wilson, *Birds, Nests and Eggs* (1814): p. 15; Wikimedia Commons: pp. 52, 54, 55, 72, 73, 104, 112, 113, 114.

Index

italic numbers refer to illustrations; **bold** to recipes